EVIDENCE FOR THE BIBLE

CONSIDER CHRISTIANITY SERIES, VOLUME 1

THIRD EDITION

ELGIN HUSHBECK, JR.

Energion Publications
Gonzalez, FL
2023

Unless otherwise noted, all scripture taken from the HOLY BIBLE, NEW INTERNATIONAL VERSION. Copyright © 1973, 1978, 1984 International Bible Society, Used by permission of Zondervan Bible Publishers.

Scriptures marked NASB are from the NEW AMERICAN STANDARD BIBLE®, Copyright © 1960, 1962, 1963, 1971, 1972, 1973, 1975, 1977, 1995 by The Lockman Foundation. Used by permission.

ISBN: 978-1-63199-862-1
eISBN: 978-1-63199-863-8
Library of Congress Control Number: 2023942304

Energion Publications
P. O. Box 841
Gonzalez, FL 32560
http://www.energionpubs.com
pubs@energion.com

To
Col. Elgin L. Hushbeck, Sr.
and
Gertrude G. Hushbeck
My Father and Mother

TABLE OF CONTENTS

Acknowledgments

As has been said, no book, especially one such as this, is a single person's work. This book results from many years of research and countless discussions. First and foremost, I want to thank my wife and family for putting up with me as I researched and wrote this book. I can say without hesitation that had it not been for their love, support, understanding, and encouragement, I could not have written this book. I want to also thank Inge Johnson for the time she has spent reading and correcting the several early drafts of this work and for the comments she has given me. My special thanks go to my readers, Starlett Ichsan Johnson, Tim Munson, David C. Rimoldi, and Steven B. Sherman. They gave me invaluable help on the final versions of this manuscript. Others who deserve to be singled out for their comments and inputs, both formal and informal, are Courtney Duncan, Brooks Thomas, Jeff Srinivasan, Tom Meehan, Rob Kursinski, Don Spitizmesser, and Joe Grahle. Much of what is good in this book is a result of their input and criticisms. Any mistakes or errors, however, are mine. In addition, I want to give a special thanks to one of my professors at Simon Greenleaf University, Dallas Willard, who, at a crucial time, encouraged me to continue and to publish. I also want to thank Roger Schmidt, one of my early professors in Religious Studies, and Sidney Allen for helping me to see things logically.

Special thanks go to Jonathan William, who read a draft of the third edition. While he often disagreed, he gave me extremely valuable feedback and suggestions, making this book better.

I would also like to thank the many people who so kindly (and even those who sometimes not so kindly) gave me feedback and comments on the earlier editions of this book. Finally, I would like to thank the many people, in particular, Larry and Diane Nixon, especially my editor Henry Neufeld, and of course, my wife, friend, and companion, Hanna, for pushing me to finish this new edition.

PREFACE TO 2ND EDITION

While God does not change, the defense of Christianity does. Critics are constantly coming up with new arguments. Actually, they usually are just dusting off old arguments long since refuted and discarded, but the net effect is the same. What was not an issue yesterday suddenly becomes the latest reason why Christianity is false.

On the other side of the spectrum is the discovery of new evidence. Researchers find new manuscripts and archaeological discoveries continue to broaden our understanding of the ancient world and support the Biblical account. I have revised this second edition considering some of these developments.

Since the first Edition of *Consider Christianity*, several new books have been published attacking the Christian faith. Most have constructed straw men, which they then proceed to knock down. Because of this, they are hard to take seriously.

One notable exception to this is Michael Martin's *The Case Against Christianity*. While Martin still fails to make his case, he has at least taken some of the defenders of Christianity seriously.

In addition, science has not stood still. In the first edition, I addressed some theories and speculations that might avoid the need for God. Some of these have since fallen by the wayside, only to be replaced by new theories and speculations.

One other development has been the publication of the results of the Jesus Seminar, whose work I referred to in the first edition when it was a work in process. The significant impact of the seminar's work has been a renewed interest in the *Gospel of Thomas*, which they have included along with the other four Gospels. In response, I added a brief discussion of the *Gospel of Thomas* in the section on the canon.

Elgin L Hushbeck, Jr
Redlands, CA
March 2005

Preface to 3rd Edition

I began writing what ultimately became this book in the mid-1980s. A lot has changed since then. In early 2000 I revised and updated this book, adding enough new material to split it into two books, this one and *Christianity and Secularism*.

Now 15 years later, with plans for an audio edition and the book being translated into other languages, my publisher and I believe it is time for a new edition.

This update was not as significant as the second edition. No splitting one book into two this time. Most of the changes involve improving my writing, as my skills have improved over the years. I added some comments here and tweaked an argument there. In a few places, I addressed nuances missed in the first two editions or which have become more relevant over the years.

The most significant changes involved updating some arguments with some recent developments. As with the second edition, these developments only supported the case for Christianity. Thus this edition adds the recent finding of Ai, mentioned in Judges, which critics saw as an error in the biblical account. I also added a brief discussion on developments in microbiology showing what Darwin thought was evolution was, in fact, devolution and limited to the biological classification of family and below.

All the recent developments since the first edition have only further strengthened the belief that Christianity is a rational, reasonable, and relevant religion.

Elgin Hushbeck
Wausau, WI
Nov 2022

How to Read this Book

The Consider Christianity Series aims to present a systematic defense of the Christian Faith, with this volume focusing on the evidence for the Bible. Because of this step-by-step approach, different people will want to read this book differently.

This book is written with non-Christians in mind and tries to address a vast range of questions and objections. Since not everyone will start this book with the same beliefs, not everyone will want to begin with Chapter 1 or even read the chapters in order.

For example, Chapter 1 deals with the text of the Bible and the Canon of Scripture, why some books are in the Bible and others are not. If this is not an issue, you may skip this chapter. In short, while this book is a step-by-step argument for the Christian faith, you might only want to read the areas where you have questions.

Below is a brief description of each chapter of the book, giving you an idea of the questions addressed so you can easily find the issues that interest you.

VOLUME I - EVIDENCE FOR THE BIBLE

ONE   *How Did We Get the Bible?*   9

What were the origins of the Bible? Did the early church councils change the Bible? Who chose the books? How do we know that the Bible has not changed in the translation process over the years? In short, do we have the Bible as the apostles and prophets wrote it?

TWO   The Bible and Modern Criticism   37

Having established the Bible had not changed, the question remains: Who wrote it? Much of modern criticism has undermined the faith of many under the guise of empirical research. This chapter examines modern critical methods and shows that many are unscientific and biased against Christianity.

Although it may be true that the Bible has come down to us intact, this means little if what the apostles and prophets wrote was wrong. In this chapter, we compare the Bible with the findings of archaeology. After discussing the problems with such comparisons, we see considerable support.

Perhaps nothing has challenged faith more than the discoveries of modern science. Are science and religion locked in mortal combat? What is the proper relationship between them? Can they exist together, or must you choose one or the other? While some conflict is inevitable, this in no way threatens the validity of either religion or science.

Having shown that science and religion need not be mortal enemies, there remains the question of whether or not modern science has shown the Bible to be false. With chapter four in mind, we look at the questions of creation and evolution. We compare the different views of the creation account in Genesis to modern science and evolution.

This chapter examines the historical reliability of the Bible. How can we tell if a document is reliable or not? After reviewing the methods used to judge historical documents. We apply these methods to the Bible, including looking at the question of contradictions. We can trust the Bible.

At this point, we have seen that the Bible we have today is the same as that written by the apostle and prophets. It accurately describes events; it does not contradict itself and has not been disproven by modern science.

All this means little if it is only the writings of men. This chapter examines prophecy in the Bible to see that no human could have written this book alone. The Bible is not just the speculations of men but the Word of God!

INTRODUCTION

'Come now, let us reason together,' says the Lord.
(Isaiah 1:18)

There are two kinds of openness, the openness of indifference... and the openness that invites us to the quest for knowledge.
(Allan Bloom)[1]

IT IS QUITE POPULAR TODAY in many circles to regard religion as a spiritual pursuit in which, while the goal may be desirable, the route is not essential. Pluralism reigns supreme. Committees seek to build bridges between the different religious traditions with harmony and coexistence keywords.

All this pluralism has not brought about a heightened awareness of our spiritual nature. It has not brought us closer to our Creator. If anything, the opposite is true. The belief that the path to God is irrelevant has, rightly or wrongly, led to the conclusion that God is irrelevant. The question arises: If it makes no difference how you get there, why go at all?

Not surprisingly, many polls show a significant decline in religious beliefs, including Christianity. A Pew Research Center poll in 2019 is typical, showing a twelve percent decline in those claiming to be Christian over the previous decade. Meanwhile, those claiming no religious belief rose by nine percent.[2]

---

1   Alan Bloom, *The Closing of the American Mind* (New York: Simon and Schuster, 1987) p. 41

2   Pew Research Center, *In U.S., Decline of Christianity Contiues at Rapid Pace* October 17, 2019, https://www.pewresearch.org/religion/2019/10/17/in-u-s-decline-of-christianity-continues-at-rapid-pace/

The only religious point of view currently shunned is the one that holds that there actually is a God who cares enough to have established a particular way of approaching Him. The idea that there are correct and incorrect ways of coming to God, that one religion is right and all the others are wrong, is repugnant to those wielding the banner of pluralism.

Since the first edition of this book, some have moved beyond indifference to an increasingly hostile attitude, actively seeking to limit and restrict traditional religious beliefs.

Attacks on all houses of worship have grown to where church security is a growing concern of clergy, and some now have armed guards. In 2007, an armed guard at the New Life Church shot and killed a man who had entered the church seeking to murder those present. He had already killed two sisters and their dad in the parking lot, along with two others and at a missionary training center earlier that day. It was not the first nor the last.

During COVID, churches were forced to remain closed in some states, even after bars and casinos were allowed to open. Secularists seek to prioritize their views over what they see as the inferior view of the religious. Religion, they claim, had no right to be in the public square. Even the right to practice one's religious belief has become common before the Supreme Court.

In 2017, the court ruled 7-2 that the State of Colorado Civil Right Commission could not force a Christian baker, Jack Phillips, to make a cake he believed violated his religious beliefs. The Court also ruled that the Commission, "disparaged Phillips' faith as despicable and characterized it as merely rhetorical, and compared his invocation of his sincerely held religious beliefs to defenses of slavery and the Holocaust." This the court ruled, "violated the State's duty under the First Amendment."

While victory for Phillips, it took five years, and it did not end the states' attempts to prosecute him. The commission brought a similar charge and as I write this, that case is on appeal.

Many consider the belief that there is only one acceptable way to God to be an arrogant position. Still, it was the position held by Jesus Christ. In the Gospel of John, He said of Himself, *"I am the way and the truth and the life. No one comes to the Father except through me"* (John 14:6). This statement is arrogant unless, of course, it is true.

Today many people consider the claims of Christianity to be outdated and old-fashioned or even dangerous and harmful. Society has outgrown its superstitious past. Science and reason provide a new foundation for civilization, in which religion is no longer needed. Yet is this so? Many polls in the U.S. show that, on average, religious people are happier.[3]

This book argues Christianity is not an outdated part of our superstitious past. When one considers all of the evidence, it is a rational, reasonable, and relevant religion. I intend to show that God exists, that he has spoken to us, and that the written record of His revelation is the Bible. The Bible has not been corrupted through the years. It is an accurate and reliable record of God's interactions, with its central message concerning the nature, purpose, and work of Jesus Christ. It is a message that has relevance for us today. In short, Christianity is not a religion created by people but a faith given by God.

The evidence for Christianity is both vast and extensive. This book is the first in a series that will present some of this evidence. This volume will limit its examination to the evidence for the Bible.

We will focus on the questions raised by critics. One of the most fundamental questions about the Bible today is how closely it conforms to what the original writers wrote between 2000 and 3000 years ago. Has it changed? Many have claimed the early church councils altered the Bible. Who chose the books? How do we know the translation process did not corrupt the Bible over the years? In short, do we have the Bible as the apostles and prophets wrote it?

---

3   Albert L. Winseman, *Faith Factor: Is a Religious Life a Happier One?* Jan 20,2004, Gallup, https://news.gallup.com/poll/10333/faith-factor-religious-life-happier-one.aspx

What about all the modern scholarship that questions many traditional views of authorship and dating? Who wrote the various books of the Bible, and when? Did Moses really write the first five books of Hebrew scripture? Did the historical Jesus say everything the Gospels attribute to him? How would we know? How can we tell?

What about the finding of modern archaeology? Haven't archaeologists raised questions about the accounts in the Bible? Then there are broader questions about the conflicts between science and religion. Are they locked in mortal combat? Must one choose between them? What is the proper relationship?

How about the specific differences between biblical accounts and modern science? Must one choose between creation and evolution? How about the age of the earth? Can the biblical account be reconciled with the current science that says the universe is 13.5 billion years old?

How can we tell if the accounts recorded in the Bible are accurate? What about all the claims that the Bible contradicts itself?

None of this matters if the Bible is just men's writings about what they think about God. Yet the Bible claims to be more than that; it claims to be the inspired word of God. How can we tell? How can we determine if the Bible actually was actually inspired by God?

This book seeks to answer these, and many more common questions critics raise. Still, no single book could ever hope to cover it all. In a book of this size, we can only begin to survey the subject. In the following pages, I will attempt to answer the most significant and common questions asked by skeptics concerning the reliability and inspiration of the Bible. I will also seek to dispel many misconceptions that have arisen through the years.

Unfortunately, answering every question would require a book so large that it would be unreadable. Since I hope people will read this book and the others in the series, I have focused the discussion on the questions often raised by critics, rather than just picking the easy ones.

Finally, this series defends fundamental historical Christianity. Christianity, particularly in the 21st century, is a vastly complex array of churches and denominations encompassing a very wide and diverse set of beliefs. This series strives to reflect a view of Christianity that the vast majority of Christians have believed in since the early church nearly 2000 years ago.

Yet, while this covers most, it does not cover all. For example, not everyone who would call themselves a Christian believes in the Trinity. Some have objected to my including this as a defining doctrine in the second book.

Because of this, Christians looking for proof or affirmation of their own personal beliefs will be disappointed. On the other hand, skeptics seeking absolute proof of things like the existence of God will not find it here.

As I will discuss in the second book of the series, *Christianity and Secularism*, and the third book, *Faith and Reason*, there is no such thing as absolute proof. As I point out in my book *Seeking Truth*, according to the current research, we cannot even prove we exist, much less anything else.

Thus, demands for absolute proof are little more than a defense mechanism. Someone can safely demand some impossible level of proof before they believe. When that level is not met, they can confidently reject it.

This book does not attempt to "argue people into the kingdom." If for nothing else, I believe that is impossible. There is a spiritual component here. Christianity is a decision one makes, not a view one is argued into holding through iron-clad logic.

The goal here is not to prove Christianity true, but to show that, when one looks at all the evidence, it has not been disproven, and it is a belief that intelligent and rational people can, and in fact, do hold in the 21st century. I happen to believe that when one does consider all the evidence, it is the best conclusion. Still, I can see how some would reach different conclusions.

As we will see, the different conclusions are driven more by the presuppositions one brings to these questions than the actual evidence, for often the evidence, while pointing one way or the other, does not demand any particular conclusion.

Ultimately, it is faith in those presuppositions that will normally drive these conclusions. But then, contrary to some skeptics, faith is a component in everything we believe, not just religious beliefs. So, if you are seeking absolute proof, you will not find it here.

Yet, this should not be taken to mean evidence is irrelevant. One does not need to start with a belief in God to look at the evidence and reach the conclusion that God exists. If that was the case, no atheist would have changed their mind. But the evidence is strong enough that some do. I am an example.

The point here is that if you start with a presupposition that basically says God is impossible, it will be extremely hard to reach any other conclusion without first questioning that presupposition. The evidence becomes effectively irrelevant, for barring absolute proof, which is itself impossible, nothing will overcome your presupposition.

Instead, all one needs is to see the question of God's existence as an open question, and then ask which way does the evidence point?

Likewise, if you are looking for affirmation of your beliefs, you will likewise be disappointed. While most Christians can agree on a core of beliefs, there are disagreements on a whole range of details. While the vast majority of Christians believe God inspired the Bible, they differ on precisely what inspiration means. This book defends the core but reflects the differences.

As a result, in some places, I will discuss the various ways Christians have answered critics and leave it to readers to choose the one they see as most acceptable.

The goal here is not to defend this or that particular set of beliefs but to defend the core gospel message, the message of the cross. That message is grounded in the Bible's teachings, so this first book begins there.

What I hope will be clear is that the weight of evidence is firmly in favor of Christianity. As we begin the twenty-first century, there remain compelling reasons to believe that the words of Jesus spoken 2000 years ago have relevance in our modern age.

1

How Did We Get the Bible?

The influence of the Bible permeates almost every aspect of life in the twentieth-century Western world. . . It is a vital part of our total cultural heritage; indeed, many people would claim that it is, for a variety of reasons, the most important and influential collection of writings ever brought together and bound in a single volume.
(John Hayes)[1]

KONSTANTIN VON TISCHENDORF was only 29 years old when he made one of the most important discoveries concerning the history of the Bible – and it started in the trash. As a student at the University of Leipzig in Germany, Tischendorf became interested in studying the New Testament's recensions or the New Testament in its earliest form.

Naturally, an essential part of his research required the examination of very early texts of the Bible. When Tischendorf began his work, only a few early copies of the New Testament existed. So, in 1844, Tischendorf set off for the Middle East.

His journey brought him to St. Catherine's monastery at the foot of Mt. Sinai. St. Catherine's was founded in A.D. 527 to commemorate the traditional site where Moses saw the burning bush. Throughout the centuries, its large granite walls have provided many with a place of safety. They also contained a library, and it was in this library that Tischendorf hoped to find some insight into the early history of the New Testament.

---

1   John Hayes, *Introduction to the Bible* (Philadelphia: Westminster Press, 1971) p. 3.

One day, Tischendorf noticed a basket full of parchments, one of the materials used when copying ancient manuscripts. When he inquired about the basket, the monks told him it contained trash they used to light their oven. There had been three baskets, but the monks had already used the first two lighting their fires.

Searching through the remaining basket, Tischendorf was surprised to find 43 leaves or pages of parchment containing some of the oldest Greek manuscripts of the Bible he had ever seen. While they let Tischendorf keep the leaves found in the trash, the monks gathered from his reaction that these old manuscripts might be valuable for something other than lighting fires.

Tischendorf returned to St. Catherine's in 1853 to look for additional manuscripts. By then, the monks were suspicious, and the trip was fruitless. In 1859, under the sponsorship of the Russian Tsar Alexander II, Tischendorf made another journey, but this time he brought a gift.

He had recently published a new edition of the Septuagint, an early Greek translation of the Hebrew Scriptures. When Tischendorf presented his Edition of the Septuagint to the monastery, the steward told him that he also had a copy. The steward then took Tischendorf back to his room to show him an ancient manuscript wrapped in a red cloth. Not only did it contain most of the Hebrew Scriptures in Greek, but the New Testament as well.

The monastery sold the manuscript to Alexander II for $7000. In 1933, the Soviet government, short on cash, sold the manuscript to the British Museum for £100,000. The manuscript found by Tischendorf is now called Codex Sinaiticus. Written between A.D. 325 and 360, it is the second oldest, nearly complete manuscript of the Bible and the oldest entire New Testament.

The work of scholars like Tischendorf have shed considerable light on the process by which the Bible came down to us. Yet, many misconceptions concerning the origin of the Bible are still prevalent.

The actress Shirley Maclaine wrote about one of the most common when she had a conversation with a friend named David concerning reincarnation and the Bible in her book, *Out on a Limb*.

> "But David," I said, "Why aren't these teachings recorded in the Bible?"
>
> "They are," he said. "The theory of reincarnation *is* recorded in the Bible. But the proper interpretations were struck from it during an Ecumenical Council meeting of the Catholic Church in Constantinople sometime around 553 A.D., called the Council of Nicaea. The Council members voted to strike those teachings from the Bible in order to solidify Church control."[2]

While David's theory would explain why the Bible does not mention reincarnation or many other such beliefs, it does have a small problem. There is no evidence to support it. Even David's description of the council where this editing supposedly took place is erroneous.

Church councils were named for the city where the Bishops gathered. In light of this fact, David's statement that a "meeting of the Catholic Church in Constantinople sometime around 553 A.D., called the Council of Nicaea," reveals a lack of understanding concerning even the most basic facts about the councils.

The council of Nicaea met in the city of Nicaea in A.D. 325, not in Constantinople in A.D. 553. Since there had already been one council meeting in Constantinople, the council that met there in A.D. 553 was, not too surprisingly, called the Second Council of Constantinople.

This misconception reemerged as the backdrop of a popular book and a major film, *The Da Vinci Code*. While such ideas make for exciting stories, they remain fiction. As we will see shortly, the belief that any of the councils altered the Bible is equally fictitious.

Another common story concerning the Bible is that it has changed over the years. Not through the deliberate editing of a church council but the slow, inevitable corruption caused by translation after translation after translation. For some, the translation process is like a party game, where a message goes around the room,

2   Shirley MacLaine, *Out on a Limb* (New York: Bantam, 1983) p. 237.

whispered from person to person. By the time the message reaches the last person in the line, it has changed dramatically.

The Bible has supposedly gone through so many translations that we can no longer be sure that what we read in the Bible is what the apostles and prophets really wrote thousands of years ago. Thomas Paine presented a form of this argument in his thesis, *The Age of Reason*,

> The continually progressive change to which the meaning of words is subject, the want of a universal language which renders translation necessary, the errors to which translations are again subject, the mistakes of copyists and printers, together with the possibility of willful alteration, are of themselves evidences that the human language, whether in speech or in print, cannot be the vehicle of the Word of God. The Word of God exists in something else.[3]

The main problem with this line of reasoning is that it completely ignores the translation process used for modern editions. When doing a new translation, the translators do not start with the last one and then update the language. Translators begin with the most reliable texts available in the original language, texts that consider the oldest manuscripts we have. Instead of "passing the message from person to person," each new translation goes back as close to the original as possible.

If Thomas Paine were correct, the older the translation, the more accurate it should be. Actually, the newer translations are slightly better than some of the older ones. This accuracy results from the discoveries made by scholars like Tischendorf, such that our understanding of the texts has vastly improved over the last few hundred years.

In addition, our understanding of ancient languages has dramatically improved as well. Some of this improvement comes from research on the languages themselves. Another factor is research into the general study of linguistics, how languages work, how they affect each other, and how they change over time.

---

3   Thomas Paine, *The Age of Reason* (Secaucus, New Jersey: Citadel Press, 1974) p. 63.

As a result, scholars can trace the development of languages like Greek, from the time of Homer, through the classical period, to the Koine period, the time Jesus lived, up to modern Greek.

At one time, scholars could tell the Greek of the New Testament differed from the classical Greek of Plato and Aristotle. Still, they did not know why, and there were many theories. Now we know that the Greek of the classical period changed as it spread throughout the Roman world, becoming what is now called Koine or common Greek.

This better understanding has not resulted in any radical changes in translations. Still, it has given us greater confidence that the text and our translations are accurate. You can see an example of this in the Hebrew Scriptures.

THE TEXT OF THE HEBREW SCRIPTURES

At the beginning of the twentieth century, the oldest complete Hebrew Scriptures written in Hebrew was the Codex Babylonicus Petropalitanus, located in Leningrad. This copy was made in A.D. 1008, over 1400 years after the last book of the Hebrew Scriptures had been written. Skeptics pointed to this significant time span as evidence that the text could not be reliable. They claimed that errors were sure to have resulted from the vast amount of copying that must have taken place during the 1400-year gap.

After about A.D. 500, copying the Hebrew Scripture was the job of the Masoretes, and it is from them that we get the name for this type of manuscript: the Masoretic texts. The Masoretic texts are generally considered the most reliable texts of the Hebrew Scriptures. They have formed the basis for most of our translations.

The Masoretes took the task of copying the Hebrew Scriptures very seriously. Because they believed they were copying the Word of God, the Masoretes made a tremendous effort to ensure that their copies were utterly free from errors.

In order to accomplish this task, the Masoretes used rigorous rituals to ensure that errors would not creep in. Rituals prescribed every detail of the copying process. So scribes only made copies on the skin of a clean animal. Rituals dictated the columns on each "page" and the length of each column (greater than 48 but less than 60). The column width needed to be 30 letters, and the scribe must use black ink. The rituals specified everything. Nothing was to be written from memory. Scribes could make copies only from an authentic copy, still in good condition.

In addition to these precautions, the Masoretes used a technique similar to modern computers to ensure data was transmitted correctly. In computers, this technique is referred to as a checksum. Put simply, the Masoretes counted everything they could. Every verse, word, and letter in each book had a number, and the scribes knew the middle word and the middle letter of each book. Even the number of times each letter of the alphabet occurred in a book was counted.[4]   Scribes could check each new copy using this information to see if they had made any errors. If the numbers did not come out right, something was wrong, and the error would be found and corrected.[5]

This attention to detail helps explain why we do not have many early manuscripts. Since the Masoretes took such care to ensure they made no errors, there was no reason to consider the older texts any better than the newer ones. In fact, the opposite was true, as the animal skins and the type of ink used meant that the older texts were prone to damage. When someone found a defect in a manuscript, rituals prescribed its destruction.

Even with all these elaborate precautions, there is still the possibility that scribes did not always follow them. Errors could still creep in. Fortunately, there are ways to check the texts' accuracy. One way is to compare the grammar used in a book to the grammar used during the period in which the book was initially written.

---

4   Gleason Archer, *A Survey of Old Testament Introduction* (Chicago: Moody Press, 1974) p. 65-6.
5   Norman Geisler & Ron Brooks, *When Skeptics Ask* (Wheaton, Illinois, Victor Books, 1990) p. 158.

As we now know, language is not static; it changes with time. This change is one of the main reasons people have problems when they try to read the *King James Version* or Shakespeare. It is not so much that these are difficult but that most people are not used to reading seventeenth-century English.

The prophets wrote over about 1000 years (1400 B.C. to 400 B.C.), and the Hebrew Scriptures reflect the types of Hebrew used during the various periods.[6] We could detect alterations as a reduction in these distinctions and a blending of styles.

Some of this occurred and can be seen in our copies. Still, throughout the Hebrew Scriptures, the scribes preserved many differences in grammar and dialect among the different books. They even kept some of the ancient forms of spelling. If anything had changed, you would think that at least the scribes would have updated the spelling to agree with the later conventions. Yet, it was not, supporting the contention that the text is accurate. It certainly rules out any systematic updating of the text.

Another check on the preservation of the Hebrew Scriptures comes from comparing the Masoretic text to the Septuagint, an early Greek translation of the Hebrew Scriptures. The Septuagint's name comes from the Latin word for 70 (*Septuaginta*), and an account claiming the translation was done by 72 scholars, six from each of the twelve tribes. Translated in the third and second centuries before Christ, the Septuagint provides a second witness to the accuracy of the Masoretic text.

Comparing the Septuagint to the Masoretic text makes it possible to judge the accuracy of each. This is especially true since, after the first century A.D., the Septuagint was preserved only by Christians and thus can be considered a separate witness. Studies of the differences between the Septuagint and Masoretic texts show that the text of the Hebrew Scripture has been remarkably preserved.

---

6   Bruce K Waltke, *The Textual Criticism of the Old Testament* in *The Expositor's Bible Commentary Vol. 1* ed. Frank E. Gaebelein (Grand Rapids, MI: Zondervan, 1979) p. 218.

There is a third witness to the accuracy of the Masoretic text, discovered by a Bedouin shepherd boy in 1947. While looking for a lost goat near the Dead Sea, he tossed a rock into a hole, hoping to flush out the goat. Instead of a goat, he heard the sound of shattering pottery. When he went down into the hole to look around, he found several jars containing ancient leather scrolls. His discovery of the Dead Sea Scrolls is one of the most important historical finds for the text of the Hebrew Scriptures.

Among the scrolls discovered were fragments and portions of every book in the Hebrew Scriptures, except the book of Esther. Also found was a complete copy of the book of Isaiah from around 150 B.C. This copy of Isaiah was over 1100 years older than any previously known Hebrew manuscript. Even with the vast amount of time between these two manuscripts, when the copy of Isaiah found among the Dead Sea Scrolls was compared to the Masoretic text we have today, the differences between the two were minimal.

Most of the differences that existed were minor spelling and grammatical differences that did not affect the meaning. A difference that was not simply a spelling or grammar variation is found in Isaiah 53:11.

In the copy of Isaiah found among the Dead Sea Scrolls, Isaiah 53:11 has the three-letter Hebrew word for light. This word does not appear in the Masoretic text. This difference is the only such variation in the whole chapter.

This additional word results in only a small difference in the meaning. The *King James Version* (KJV), which follows the Masoretic text, reads as follows,

> He shall see of the travail of his soul, and shall be satisfied: by his knowledge shall my righteous servant justify many; for he shall bear their iniquities.

The *New International Version* (NIV), which is the version quoted in this book, follows the Dead Sea scrolls at this point and reads,

> After the suffering of his soul, he will see the light
> of life and be satisfied; by his knowledge my righteous
> servant will justify many and he will bear their iniquities.

As you can see, while the NIV is a little clearer, there is no significant difference between these two translations.[7]

Thus by comparing the Masoretic text, the Septuagint, and the Dead Sea Scrolls, scholars can be very confident the Hebrew text used in translating modern Bibles is so close to the originals as to be, for all practical purposes, the same as that written down by the prophets. To date, no ancient manuscript discovery has ever called into question any of the doctrines of the Church. In fact, the opposite is true. The more manuscripts we find, the more they have confirmed the accuracy of the present text.

THE TEXT OF THE NEW TESTAMENT

When we examine the New Testament, we find the evidence for it to be even stronger than that for the Hebrew Scriptures. As mentioned above, the oldest complete New Testament is the Codex Sinaiticus. Written about the same time, Codex Vaticanus is a nearly complete copy. Located in the Vatican, it is believed to have been copied around A.D. 325. Codex Sinaiticus and Vaticanus show that within a few hundred years, Christians gathered the New Testament books, along with the Hebrew Scriptures, as a complete unit.

Looking at portions of the New Testament, we move even closer to the originals. While there are many controversies and even some guesswork when it comes to dating early manuscripts, most scholars believe that the oldest fragment of the New Testament is the John Rylands Manuscript, containing a portion of the book of John (18:31-33, 37-38). This fragment dates from about A.D. 125-

---

7   If anything, the "light of life" is a reference to resurrection. Since this verse is generally considered by Christians as referring to Jesus Christ as the suffering servant, this would only serve to support Christianity.

130,[8] less than 40 years after John wrote it.[9] Researchers continue to find other early manuscripts of the Bible.

In 1972, the papyrologist Jose O'Callaghan claimed that a small manuscript fragment found among the Dead Sea Scrolls (called 7Q5) was actually from the Gospel of Mark (Mark 6:52-53). Since the caves were sealed in A.D. 68, the date of the manuscript is somewhere between A.D. 50 and A.D. 68.

If correct, this would be truly astounding since the range of dates for Mark is from the mid-40s to the mid-70s, with most scholars dating Mark during the 60s. Not surprisingly, O'Callaghan's identification caused a lot of controversy. Other New Testament scholars largely rejected O'Callahan's date. The manuscript fragment was too small to make such an identification, and the date is just too early.

The case for the identification of 7Q5 with Mark received some support when scholars examined the fragment using special equipment. Much of the dispute turns on the identification of a damaged letter.

If the damaged letter is the Greek letter nu (N), then the text would be consistent with the text of Mark. The problem is the letter is missing much of the right-hand portion. To some, it looks like the letter iota (I), which would not match the text of Mark.

Recent examinations using advanced technology showed that the disputed letter is nu. It is consistent with the text of Mark, but is it the text of Mark? As a result, among papyrologists, those specifically trained in this area, there is growing support for O'Callaghan's identification.[10]

---

8   Dates for this fragment range from A.D. 95. to A.D. 130.

9   This is based on the traditional date for John of A.D. 90 - 100. A few scholars are now suggesting that John may have been written as early as A.D. 55, which would be about 70 year before the John Rylands Manuscript was made, and only about 25 years after the resurrection of Jesus.

10   For a discussion of the issues surrounding these texts and the arguments for an early date see: Cartsen Thiede & Matthew D'Ancona, *Eyewitness to Jesus* (New York: Doubleday, 1996).

In late 1994, Carsten Thiede, Director of the Institute for Basic Epistemological Research in Paderborn, Germany, announced a startling discovery about a different manuscript. Thiede dated the Magdalen papyrus, which contains portions of the Gospel of Matthew (26:7-8, 10, 14-15, 22-23, 31), to A.D. 66 or slightly earlier.[11]

As with O'Callaghan's identification of 7Q5 with Mark, this has caused considerable controversy. Before Thiede's proposed identification, the range of dates for Matthew was from the 40s to the 90s. Most liberal scholars dated Matthew in the 70s, and most conservative scholars dated it in the 60s. However, some proposed dates are as early as the 40s.

A significant aspect of the Magdalen fragments is that they are from a codex, similar to a book, and not a scroll. A codex indicates that the Magdalen fragments are at least second-generation copies and points to how rapidly the Gospels were copied and spread throughout the Roman world. As we will see shortly, this is important for establishing their reliability.

So again, the dates given by Thiede seem too early. While not impossible, they seem unlikely given the short timespans between the writing of these Gospels and the manuscripts' proposed date.

Whether the work of O'Callaghan, Thiede, and others who support the early date of these and other manuscripts stands up to the examination of scholars, what is clear is that the textual evidence for the New Testament is far and away more substantial than for any other ancient work.

Researchers continue to find manuscripts, and currently, there are around 5500[12] early Greek manuscripts and manuscript por-

---

For the arguments against the early date see: G. Stanton, *Gospel Truth? New Light on Jesus and the Gospels* (London, 1995).

11   For a discussion of the issues surrounding these texts and the arguments for an early date see: Cartsen Thiede & Matthew D'Ancona, *Eyewitness to Jesus* (New York: Doubleday, 1996)
For the arguments against the early date see: G. Stanton, *Gospel Truth? New Light on Jesus and the Gospels* (London, 1995)

12   Some manuscript portions are separate fragments from the same manuscript that were acquired at different times. As such, this number is

tions of the New Testament. These manuscripts, along with about 20,000 translations, which include over 10,000 copies of the Latin Vulgate, provide a genuinely phenomenal record of the text of the New Testament.[13]

As a comparison, let us look at a few other ancient works. About 100 years before the New Testament was written, Julius Caesar wrote his account of the Gaulic Wars. We have about ten copies of this work, made about 1000 years after Caesar wrote them. We have about seven copies of the works of Plato that date approximately 1200 years after Plato died. For any single work of Aristotle, we have about 50 copies, written about 1400 years after his death.[14]

The text of the New Testament is better established than any of these works. We have tens of copies made a thousand years later for most ancient writers. We have thousands of copies of the New Testament, beginning tens of years after they were written.

Besides the thousands of early manuscripts of the New Testament, we also have another way by which we can confirm these texts. The early church fathers wrote frequently, and they often quoted scripture when they did. We could reconstruct nearly the entire New Testament from these early quotations. These quotes act as a second witness for the text.

This evidence is why we can say those claiming the Bible has been rewritten or edited by this or that church council are simply not supported by the evidence. While the church councils began in the fourth century, we have copies of the Bible and the writings of the church fathers starting no later than the early part of the second century.

---

not the total number of manuscripts. While the exact number of separate manuscripts is not known for certain, it is around 5000.

13 Bruce M. Metzger, *The Text of the New Testament, 3rd ed.* (New York: Oxford University Press, 1992) p. 262.

14 Josh McDowell, *Evidence That Demands a Verdict* (San Bernardino, CA: Here's Life, 1979) pp. 39-41 and Gordon D. Fee, *The Textual Criticism of the New Testament* in *The Expositor's Bible Commentary Vol. 1* ed. Frank E. Gaebelein (Grand Rapids, MI: Zondervan, 1979) p. 218.

If the councils had made any changes, they would be very easy to find. We would only have to compare the copies of the Bible made before the councils to those after, and any changes would instantly become apparent. There are no signs that the text of the New Testament was systematically altered, much less altered to remove the teaching of reincarnation or any other doctrines.

Even with this evidence, some point to the missing originals and the resulting gap to the earliest manuscripts. For them, however small, this gap is evidence of unreliability. Critics claim that without the originals, we can never be sure someone did not change the text. The problem with such claims is that we do not have a single line of manuscripts but many parallel lines, each confirming the others.

Figure 1.1 shows an example of this. From a single original, many copies were made and distributed. Scribes later made second, third, and fourth-generation manuscripts from the first generation. Many of these manuscripts were lost with time.

Suppose that today, only three manuscripts remain (mss #1, #2, & #3), all fourth-generation copies. Does this mean we cannot be sure of the text before the fourth generation? Not at all. We can determine how accurately the text was copied by comparing these manuscripts.

When two manuscripts agree, the reading they have in common must be earlier than the manuscripts themselves, reflecting the common source. In our example, when mss #2 and #3 agree, they reflect a reading found in the first-generation manuscripts. When all three agree, they reflect the reading found in the original.

This example demonstrates a critical concept: there is a difference between a manuscript's date and the date of a reading found in the manuscript. That scribes copied a particular manuscript in the second century does not mean that the text it contains is from the second century. This difference between the date of the reading and the manuscript is very important in bridging the gap.

The books of the New Testament were copied and distributed widely during the apostles' lifetime. They would have resisted any

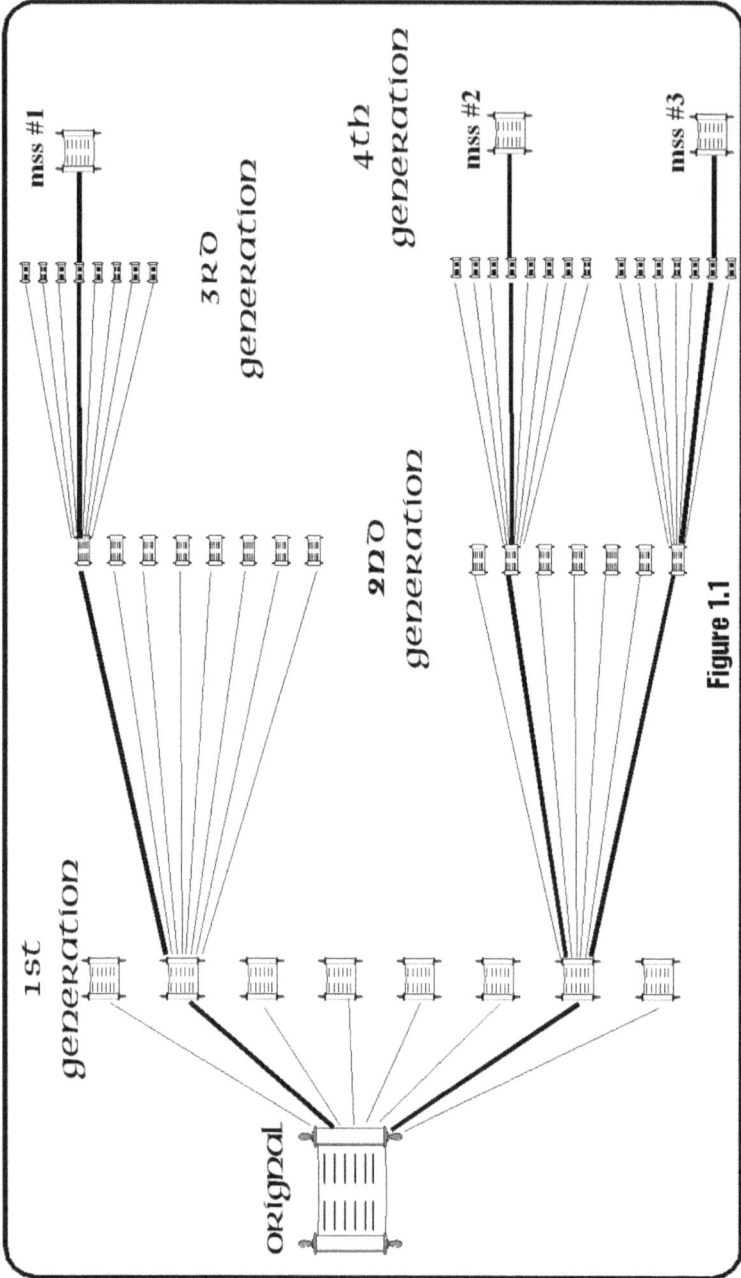

Figure 1.1

early changes. We can see in the New Testament the apostles warning against those who would bring another Gospel. (e.g., Galatians 1:8) While these warnings are about changes to their message rather than manuscripts, the principle is the same.

In addition, while they do not exist today, there are ancient accounts mentioning the preservation of the original documents into the second century.[15] One account mentions the original Gospel of John still existing in the fourth. This means some manuscripts we have today overlap with the time when the originals still existed. The evidence is strong that early Christians were concerned about preserving the books that became the New Testament.

By John's death at the end of the first century, copies were already spreading throughout the Roman world. To change them all and eliminate the originals would have required tremendous effort. As a result, those claiming the text has been deliberately changed must face a major problem with their theory.

To successfully change all the texts of the Bible would have required a significant organized effort. Yet, no such organization existed in the early Church. By the time the Church reached anything approaching the needed organizational level, it would have been well past the date of our earliest manuscripts. Even if an organized effort had been able to change the Bible, they could not have revised manuscripts already lost and only rediscovered in the last two centuries. As such, these early manuscripts show that no such editing occurred.

One final problem is that early Christians considered the Word of God sacred, and many died to protect it. For example, in 303 A.D., the Roman Emperor Diocletian ordered the destruction of all Christian scripture. While some Christians complied with the Emperor's order, many suffered torture and martyrdom to protect God's word.

---

15 Daniel B. Wallace, *Did the Original New Testament Manuscripts still exist in the Second Century?* Bible.org, Jan 21, 2009, https://bible.org/article/did-original-new-testament-manuscripts-still-exist-second-century.

After Diocletian's persecution failed, the reaction of Christians against those who had turned over scripture to the Romans was so strong that it caused controversy. Could they be forgiven? The answer was yes, but this controversy within the Church lasted for many years. As a result, a new word entered our vocabulary. Those who turn over the word of God were called "those who delivered," in Latin, *traditores.* This word has come into English as traitor.

The idea that roughly twenty years after Diocletian's persecution, at the very time that the Church was struggling with how to deal with the *traditores,* the church councils would have rewritten the Bible without leaving any trace and without anyone complaining is simply impossible. There were too many Christians throughout the world who were willing to suffer and even die to protect scripture. Many had recently done just that.

While it is clear there was no systematic effort to rewrite the New Testament books, the copying process remains an issue. The New Testament did not have the benefit of the ritual used in the Hebrew Bible. Even professional scribes could make mistakes, and it is pretty clear not all the manuscripts we have were copied by highly trained scribes. Those making copies made mistakes, and the manuscripts do have some differences. These differences are not the result of a rewrite but a copyist error.

We do see corrections in the ancient manuscripts. In fact, at Hebrews 1:3 in Codex Vaticanus, you can see where a scribe corrected the original text, only to have an even later scribe restore the original reading. In addition, he added a note in the margin, "Fool and Nave, can't you leave the old reading alone, and not alter it!"[16] It appears the first corrector was right.

Some try to make a great deal of these differences, but even Bart Ehrman, one of the leading critics, admits,

---

16   Bruce M. Metzger, *Manuscripts of the Greek Bible* (New York, Oxford Press, 1981) p. 74.
You can also see in the online digital verion at: https://digi.vatlib.it/view/MSS_Vat.gr.1209.

> most of them are completely insignificant, imma-
> terial, and of no real importance for anything other than
> showing that scribes could not spell or keep focused any
> better than the rest of us.[17]

As such, most of the time, these errors are easy to detect. While going back and forth, from original to copy, a scribe accidentally skipped to the following line, leaving several words out. In such cases, it is pretty easy to detect this by looking at the many manuscripts. But not all errors are so straightforward.

As a result, there are still some questions concerning the text in a few places. These questions arise when there are minor differences between the various ancient manuscripts, and scholars are unsure which one is the original and which is the mistake.

Scholars who evaluate the thousands of manuscripts, translations, and quotations and attempt to assemble the original text are called textual critics. For the vast majority of the Bible, probably over 95 percent, there is no doubt concerning the ancient reading of the text. In those passages where some question remains, the differences found among the various manuscripts are minor and have no effect on the teachings of the Church, regardless of which reading is correct.

Even here, there is no secrecy or attempt to deceive. Both primary Greek texts of the New Testament give the reader what scholars believe is the original text of the New Testament.[18] Interestingly, even though different groups of scholars prepared these Greek New Testaments, the text of the New Testament is identical.

In addition to the text, they include the variations, listing the manuscripts containing them and the church fathers quoting them. This information is accessible to even those with only a limited knowledge of New Testament Greek.

---

17 Bart Ehrman, *Misquoting Jesus: The Story Behind Who Changed the Bible and Why* (New York, HarperOne, 2007) p. 208.

18 The two major Greek texts of the New Testament are the Nestle-Aland Novum Testamentum Graece and the United Bible Society's The Greek New Testament.

Of course, when translators make a new version, a choice must be made between the different, or variant, readings. Because of this, many modern translations include the alternative readings in footnotes.

An example of this is Matthew 15:5-6. The New International Version translates this verse as, (Note: Subscript numbers represent the verse numbers.)

> ₅But you say that if a man says to his father or mother, "Whatever help you might otherwise have received from me is a gift devoted to God," ₆he is not to "honor his father" with it.

The footnote states that some manuscripts read: "he is not to 'honor his father *or his mother*' with it." As you can see, while the reading is different, it makes no difference to the passage's meaning. Jesus said mother at the beginning of verse 5. So the only real question is in verse 6, did he use father as a summary for father and mother, or did he explicitly mention both?

The question is somewhat different from the textual critic's point of view. Which mistake did the scribes make? Is it more likely that a scribe would mistakenly drop the word mother? Is it more likely a scribe added it since Jesus said mother earlier, perhaps thinking that an earlier scribe mistakenly left it out?

If you suspect I have chosen a simple passage as an example, it is easy to check this for yourself. All you need do is to look through one of the many modern translations that include the variant readings in footnotes and compare these to the readings found in the text.

If you don't trust the translations, you could learn Koine Greek. You can even check the manuscripts, as many are available online, including Codex Sinaiticus and Codex Vaticanus. None of this is hidden.

It has been my experience that the vast majority of these variant readings make no difference at all, much less a difference that would affect the teachings of the Bible.

In a tiny number of cases, the difference is significant enough to change the passage's meaning. Perhaps the most well-known example of this is 1 John 5:7-8. The New International Version translates these verses as (Note: Superscript numbers represent the verse numbers.)

> 7For there are three that testify: 8the Spirit, the water and the blood; and the three are in agreement.

The accompanying footnote points out that in a few very late Greek manuscripts (sixteenth century or later), the verse reads as follows,

> 7For there are three that testify *in heaven: The Father, the Word and the Holy Spirit, and these three are one. And there are three that testify on earth:* 8the Spirit, the water and the blood; and the three are in agreement. (Added text is in Italics)

This change is significant, changing the meaning of the verse. The added words are an apparent reference to the Trinity. Still, the shorter reading does not deny the Trinity; instead, it does not mention the doctrine.

One can trace the history of the passage in the manuscript evidence. The additional words are not mentioned until the 4th century when a church father writing in Latin mentions them. Then they begin to appear, first in the margins of a few Latin translations. Then in the text, most likely when a scribe mistook the margin note as a correction.

When Erasmus began producing Greek versions of the Bible in the early 16th century, others noticed that this passage was missing from the few manuscripts Erasmus used for his Greek edition. Shortly after that, a Greek version containing the disputed words was produced.

It is important to note that regardless of which reading is the original, and it is undoubtedly the shorter version, this variant does not alter the overall teachings of the Bible in any way.

One can see the teaching of the Trinity throughout the New Testament and, to some extent, in the Hebrew Scriptures. It does not depend on a single verse. No significant Christian teaching depends on a single verse, much less a verse with a variant reading.

The recent discoveries of researchers, and the work of textual critics, have shown that the text of the Bible is thoroughly reliable. They show that, despite claims to the contrary, the text of the Bible has not been changed or altered to distort the original message.

The ancient manuscripts reveal some minor issues, and almost all have clear answers. Translators address these in modern versions. Still, the large number of these manuscripts mainly confirmed the accuracy of the overall text. As a result, the text of the New Testament we have today is, for all practical purposes, the same as it was when the apostles wrote it.

THE CANON OF THE HEBREW SCRIPTURE

There is still the question of why the books found in the Bible are there while others are not. Once again, critics charge that at one of those infamous councils, church leaders got together and selected all the books they liked while rejecting all the books they didn't. As with the other charges, these also lack evidence to support them.

When Jesus quoted from the Hebrew Scripture, he did not base his arguments on the strength of a council's decision. It is very clear from the way that Jesus spoke of the Hebrew Scriptures that he considered them to be the inspired words of God.[19]

As the inspired words of God, they were authoritative and belonged to the canon of scripture from the moment the prophet wrote them. While this may explain why these books belong in the Hebrew Scriptures, it still leaves the question of how they were determined to be inspired.

In their book, *A General Introduction to the Bible,*[20] Norman Geisler and William Nix cite five principles used to test whether or

---

19   See John W. Wenham, *Christ's View of Scripture* in Inerrancy, ed. by Norman L. Geisler (Grand Rapids, MI: Academie Books, 1980) pp. 1-36.

20   Norman Geisler and William Nix, *A General Introduction to the Bible* (Chicago: Moody Press, 1986) pp. 223-231.

not God inspired a book. To be considered inspired, a book must have been written by a man of God. It should be confirmed by an act of God, a miracle, or a prophecy. It should be in agreement with other writings of God in its teachings. It should have the power of God; that is, it should impact people's lives. And lastly, it should be accepted and used by God's people.

For the Hebrew Scriptures, Jewish people determined the canon. While the exact time the canon became settled is unknown, it seems to have been early and done by consensus. The Jewish people saw the five books of Moses as Scripture from the beginning. One sees references to them as authoritative throughout the Hebrew Scriptures.[21]

Most prophets were probably accepted when they were written or shortly after. The prophet Jeremiah, in Jeremiah 7:25, written before the fall of Jerusalem in 586 B.C., speaks of prophets that God had sent earlier. Daniel, who wrote during the exile,[22] states that he "*understood from the Scriptures, according to the word of the LORD given to Jeremiah the prophet*" (Daniel 9:2).

By the time of Christ, the Jewish people knew the canon of the Hebrew Scriptures. Flavius Josephus, a Jewish historian who wrote in the later part of the first century, describes it. Josephus wrote,

> every one is not permitted of his own accord to
> be a writer, nor is there any disagreement in what is

---

21   For examples see: Joshua 8:31, Judges 1:20, 1 Kings 2:3, Ezra 6:18, Daniel 9:13, Malachi 4:4.

22   Liberal scholars, troubled by Daniel's extremely accurate prophecies, have attempted to date Daniel in the middle part of the second century B.C. This attempt has not been successful. Daniel's accurate use of Babylonian terminology, unknown in the second century B.C., and his accurate description of Babylonian court life, support Daniel's claim to be written during the exile. Also, the discovery of fragments of Daniel among the Dead Sea Scrolls which date from the middle of the second century B.C. (about the time liberal scholars claim Daniel was written), strongly argues against such a late date. For a complete discussion see: Gleason L. Archer, Jr., *Daniel in The Expositor's Bible Commentary*, ed. Frank E. Gaebelein (Grand Rapids, Michigan: Regency, 1985) pp. 4-6 and 12-26.

written; they being only prophets that have written the
original and earliest accounts of things as they learned
them from God himself by inspiration; and others have
written what hath happened in their own times, and
that in a very distinct manner also. For we have not an
innumerable multitude of books among us, disagree-
ing from and contradicting one another [as the Greeks
have], but only twenty-two books, which contain the
records of all the past times; which are justly believed
to be divine.[23]

The 22 books mentioned by Josephus are the same as the 39
books we have in the Hebrew Scripture today. The difference in the
two numbers results from Josephus counting some books as one,
whereas today, they are two or more. For example, Josephus counted the twelve minor prophets as one book since they were kept
together on a single scroll. Josephus also counted Samuel, Kings,
and Chronicles as single books. In contrast, in modern Bibles, each
comprises two books.

From the beginning, the Jewish people saw the Temple as the
center of their faith. Following the Temple's destruction in A.D.
70, many Jewish leaders believed they needed to establish their
scripture's canon. With the Temple gone, the Hebrew Scriptures
were to become the center.

So the Jewish leaders met in the city of Jamnia in A.D. 90.
The books they chose were the same as those mentioned earlier
by Josephus and the same that we have in our Bibles today. The
discussions at Jamnia centered around just a few books, such as
Esther and the Song of Songs. They accepted, without question,
most books in the Hebrew Scriptures. Rather than pick and choose
the books that best suited them, the Jewish leaders ratified those
books that the Jewish people already accepted as the Word of God.
They did not add or remove any books.

---

23 Flavius Josephus, Flavius Josephus Against Apion in *The Works of Flavius
    Josephus Vol. 4* trans. William Whiston, (Grand Rapids, MI: Baker Books,
    1979) p. 158.

THE CANON OF THE NEW TESTAMENT

When we come to the New Testament, like the manuscript evidence, the evidence for the canon is even greater than for the Hebrew Scripture. By Peter's death, which occurred no later than A.D. 68,[24] some of the apostles' writings were already accepted as scripture. In the second letter Peter wrote, he states,

> [15]Bear in mind that our Lord's patience means salvation, just as our dear brother Paul also wrote you with the wisdom that God gave him. [16]He writes the same way in all his letters, speaking in them of these matters. His letters contain some things that are hard to understand, which ignorant and unstable people distort, as they do the other Scriptures, to their own destruction. (2 Peter 3:15-16)

Here Peter clearly sees the writings of Paul on an equal footing with the "*other Scriptures.*" The apostle Paul, writing at about the same time, refers to a passage in the Gospel of Luke as Scripture.[25]

Through the writings of the church fathers during the first 300 years of church history, one can trace the development of the canon. Most books were accepted very early and not seriously questioned afterward. By the end of the first century, Christians were collecting the letters of Paul. Around A.D. 160, Tatian combined the four Gospels into a single unit called the *Diatessaron.*

Much of the push to establish a canon came about as a reaction to Marcion. Marcion was a wealthy ship-owner who moved to Rome in A.D. 140 and joined the Christian community there. Extremely anti-Semitic, Marcion rejected anything Jewish. Around A.D. 140, he produced his own version of the canon. Unsurprisingly, he threw out the entire Hebrew Scripture and three of the four Gospels. The Gospel of Luke was acceptable to him, but only after it had been "cleaned up" to remove all Jewish references.

Marcion's version of the canon was clearly unacceptable and self-serving. Still, it raised the question: If his canon was wrong,

---

24 Peter was martyred during the rule of the Nero who ruled from A.D. 54 - 68.

25 1 Timothy 5:18 quotes Deuteronomy 25:4 and Luke 10:7, referring to both as Scripture.

which books made up the actual canon? A manuscript from about
A.D. 170-180 describes the canon as it began to take shape. Called
the Muratorian Canon, after its discoverer, Lodovica Muratori, the
manuscript contains a description of the books most Christians
considered scripture.

The list is very close to the books we find in the New Testament today. The books of *Hebrews, 1&2 Peter,* and *3 John* were not
mentioned. *The Revelation of Peter* is listed as questionable, while
The Shepherd of Hermas is rejected.[26]

The discussion within the Church concerning the contents of
the canon continued. While Christians accepted most books, a few
were still being discussed. Around A.D. 300, Eusebius compiled a
list of books under consideration.

He divided the books into three categories. In the category of
Homologoumena – those books accepted by all – he placed most of
the books in the New Testament (the four Gospels, *Acts*, the letters
of Paul, *1 Peter, 1 John,* and the book of *Revelation)*. The remaining
books of the New Testament, Eusebius placed in the category of
amphiballomena – books disputed by some but *"recognized by most
churchmen."*[27] All other books that had at one time been considered
but did not appear in the New Testament, Eusebius placed in the
notha – spurious writings category. By the council of Carthage,
A.D. 397, the Western Church had reached enough of a consensus
over the form of the canon to approve a list of books identical to
today.

THE GOSPEL OF THOMAS

While settled for over a thousand years, some recently renewed
the charge that the early Christians left out some books out of the
Bible. The book most frequently cited along these lines is the *Gospel*

---

26 *Encyclopedia Britannica 15th ed., s.v. Biblical Literature* by H. Grady
    Davis, p. 940.
27 Tim Dowley ed. *Eerdmans' Handbook to the History of Christianity*
    (Carmel, New York: Guideposts, 1977) p. 105.

of Thomas, found among a whole library of Gnostic documents discovered at Nag Hammadi, Egypt, in 1954.

Gnosticism refers to various religious movements popular during the 2nd century. They get their name from the Greek word *gnosis,* which means 'to know.' Most of these religious movements claimed special or secret knowledge, a knowledge that led them to the truth. The early Church strongly opposed Gnosticism. John wrote his three letters, the last New Testament letters, in opposition to early Gnostics.

The *Gospel of Thomas* is certainly Gnostic in origin. Unlike the other Gospels, which record many details of the life of Christ, the *Gospel of Thomas* is just a collection of 114 sayings of Jesus, saying supposedly secretly revealed to Thomas. As Craig Blomberg has pointed out, "Many of the sayings have a patently Gnostic flavor."[28]

While many sayings are gnostic in origin, over half are similar to those found in the Bible. Since the Gospel contains no details of Jesus' life, some have suggested that *Thomas* may be earlier than the four Gospels in the Bible. Some think it may have even been a source for the others. These claims have led some to see *Thomas* as an authentic Gospel, and the *Jesus Seminar* recently published it along with the other four. We will have more on the *Jesus Seminar* in the next chapter.

Despite its recent popularity, there are strong reasons to question the authenticity of *The Gospel of Thomas.* First and foremost would be its gnostic teachings, which are incompatible with the teachings of the New Testament. While some might claim that perhaps *Thomas* represents the actual teachings of Jesus, there are problems with this.

First, unlike the Gospels found in the New Testament, no scholar would argue that the apostle Thomas wrote the *Gospel of Thomas.* In addition, it would appear that the writer of *Thomas* used the Gospels as sources. As Blomberg points out,

---

28   Craig Blomberg, *The Historical Reliability of the Gospels* (Downers Grove, Illinois: Inter-Varsity, 1987) p. 209.

> Where Thomas parallels the four gospels it is un-
> likely that any of the distinctive elements in Thomas
> predates the canonical versions. In a number of cases
> these distinctives reappear in the Coptic translations of
> the New Testament, which no one would claim reflects
> independent sources of information about Jesus. . . It
> is hard to avoid the conclusion that the author of the
> Gospel of Thomas knew the New Testament Gospels
> as they now stand, even if he may have quoted them
> fairly loosely. [29]

Thus, there appears to be little to argue for the *Gospel of Thomas* as part of the canon. One thing is clear from the writings of the early church fathers: they considered scripture to be a very narrow classification of books.

They accepted only those books that could meet the strict standards. They did not simply pick the books they liked and reject those they didn't. *The Shepherd of Hermas*, for example, was a book many in the early Church praised and encouraged people to read and study. Yet, while they liked the book, it did not qualify as scripture and thus was not included in the canon. Therefore the question is not why the early Church rejected *The Gospel of Thomas* but why should it be accepted?

Conclusion

There is little evidence to support the skeptics' claims that the Bible has been changed or altered by church councils or that the translation process has corrupted it. In light of the evidence, it becomes very difficult to hold any position other than the text we have today is essentially the same as that penned by the authors.

For the development of the canon, we find it developed quite early, not behind the closed doors of some church council, but among an open discussion of the Church as a whole, beginning long before the councils.

Once the councils started, they only ratified the canon; they did not create it. Only after the Church had agreed on the canon

---

29   Craig Blomberg, *The Historical Reliability of the Gospels* (Downers Grove, Illinois: Inter-Varsity, 1987) p. 211.

did the councils even take up the issue. When we examine the Bible, we can do so with the confidence that it is complete. Nowhere do we find evidence of any changes, additions, or omissions that would, in any way, affect the teachings of the Bible.

2

THE BIBLE
AND MODERN CRITICISM

*First of all, you must understand
that in the last days scoffers will come.*
(2 Peter 3:3)

FROM ALL OVER THE COUNTRY, they came to meet twice a year for six years. It would not last very long. They would meet for just a weekend, discuss, debate, and then on Sunday, they would vote. Instead of ballots, they used beads. Red, pink, gray, and black beads dropped into a ballot box. The meetings were part of the *Jesus Seminar.* They were voting on whether Jesus actually said what the Gospels attributed to him.

The *Jesus Seminar,* a group of 200 biblical scholars, was founded in 1985 by Robert Funk, former president of the Society of Biblical Literature. Its purpose was to counteract fundamentalist and evangelical views of a literal reading of the Bible, so the colored beads represented the varying levels of certainty concerning the sayings of Jesus.

Red indicated that the expression was authentic, and pink meant that Jesus might have said something similar. Gray meant that, while the ideals may have come from Jesus, the words did not, while black signified that the saying did not come from Jesus.

At one such meeting in Atlanta during the Fall of 1988, 24 scholars met to decide whether or not Jesus said the Lord's Prayer. After discussing the issue at the weekend gathering, they held the vote. Based on the tally of the beads, they decided that Jesus had not spoken the Lord's Prayer.

When they finished their last meeting in 1991, the scholars of the Jesus Seminar placed 30 percent of the sayings recorded in the Bible into the gray category and 50 percent into the black. They believed that only 20 percent of the sayings of Jesus recorded in the Bible were the words, or close to the words, that Jesus had actually spoken.[1]

While the conclusion of 200 scholars may seem impressive, the results of the Jesus Seminar raise several questions. How do these scholars know this? How can they determine, 2000 years later, what Jesus did or did not say? On what basis did these scholars conclude that Jesus said, "Blessed are you who are poor, for yours is the kingdom of God" (Luke 6:20), and yet did not say, "Blessed are you when people insult you, persecute you and falsely say all kinds of evil against you because of me" (Matthew 5:11)? How do they know that Jesus did not say the Lord's Prayer?

In the last chapter, we mentioned that the textual critics' job is to evaluate the many early Bible manuscripts to determine the original text. This type of scholarship is only one part of biblical criticism. Textual criticism, also referred to as lower criticism, is generally accepted by conservative and liberal scholars as a valuable tool for understanding the Bible. As the term lower criticism implies, there is another type of biblical criticism that, as one might expect, is referred to as higher criticism.

According to Samuel Sandmel, whose book on the Hebrew Scripture claims to be "unabashedly a book of higher criticism," higher criticism is "the study of the meaning, significance, origin, and purpose of the writings."[2]

While conservative and liberal scholars generally agree on the methods and findings of lower criticism, there is vast disagreement regarding higher criticism. A significant reason for the disagreement is that, unlike lower criticism, which deals mainly with facts, the

---

1   John Dart, *Seminar Rules Out 80% of Words Attributed to Jesus Los Angeles Times*, March 4, 1991, p. A1, A24.

2   Samuel Sandmel, *The Herew Scriptures* (New York: Oxford University Press, 1978) p. 18.

thousands of manuscripts to compare and evaluate, higher criticism must rely primarily on theories and assumptions to reach its conclusions. The difference between the theories and assumptions of Liberal and Conservative scholars leads them to their different conclusions.

A clear example of the different assumptions scholars make occurs in dating books of the Bible. A standard dating technique of higher criticism that scholars commonly use with ancient literature is to determine if a book contains any anachronisms or references to a time later than the supposed date of the book.

Suppose we had a letter allegedly written by George Washington. While reading the letter, we find a reference to the Civil War. In this case, we would know that George Washington could not have written it because he died over sixty years before the Civil War began. We would have to conclude that the letter was a forgery and that someone else wrote it after the Civil War.

While this principle works fine for a letter written by George Washington, can it be applied to the writings of the apostles and prophets? Here is where conservative and liberal scholars begin to go down separate paths. A liberal scholar would say that this is a standard tool of scholarship, and as such, they can and should use it with the Bible.

Isaiah 44:28 states King Cyrus will allow the rebuilding of the Temple. When liberal scholars examine this passage, they conclude that Isaiah did not write it. He lived before the Temple was even destroyed, much less rebuilt.

On the other hand, Conservative scholars have no problem with such passages because they are prophetic. Isaiah was not saying that Cyrus *had* allowed the rebuilding of the Temple, but that he *would* allow the reconstruction of the Temple.

Of course, Isaiah mentioned this over a hundred years before it occurred; he claimed to be a prophet, not a historian. If one accepts the possibility of predictive prophecy, then its occurrence in the writings of a prophet should not present a problem. One should expect a prophet to be prophetic.

This difference reveals one of the main disagreements between liberal and conservative scholars. Liberal scholars approach the Bible as simply a collection of writings. They do not see the authors as inspired by God but as expressing their personal and collective convictions concerning God.

As a result, liberal scholars automatically reject anything supernatural in the Bible, such as prophecies or miracles. This rejection is independent of any evidence. Where prophecies and miracles do occur, the scholar must somehow explain them away. The German scholars Franz H. R. von Frank and Paul Schaarschmidt wrote,

> The representation of a course of history is a priori to be regarded as untrue and unhistorical if supernatural factors interpose in it. Everything must be naturalized and likened to the course of natural history.[3]

Conservative scholars have no such limitations. They believe that God inspired those who wrote the Bible. Prophecies and miracles are evidence that the Bible is inspired and confirms its divine origins. Instead of the evidence, often it is the different assumptions scholars make that lead them to different conclusions.[4]

During the latter part of the nineteenth century, Christianity was on the ropes in an intellectual sense. The Bible and science seemed to conflict in many places. Archaeologists of the time claimed that the Bible contained many errors. Reason and religion were seen as directly competing with each other, and scholars were, to a large extent, called upon to accept one or the other. There was an assumption that still exists today for some that "real" scholars do not believe in the Bible. If someone believes in the Bible, they are obviously not a "real" scholar.

---

3   Frank, *Geshichte und Kritik der Neuren Theologie* quoted in Josh McDowell, *Evidence That Demands a Verdict Vol. II* (San Bernardino, CA: Here's Life Pub., 1975) p. 7.

4   It is important to note that scholars need not assume that the writers of the Bible were inspired by God. A scholar need only leave the question of the supernatural open and examine the evidence for alleged occurrences to see if they are supported.

Around the end of the nineteenth century, this debate occurred in many seminaries. The resulting conflict was between those subjugating their beliefs concerning the Bible to the emerging fields of science and those who continued accepting the Bible as the Word of God. To a large extent, this battle centered around the authorship of the first five books of the Bible and a theory called the Documentary Hypothesis.

THE DOCUMENTARY HYPOTHESIS

Traditionally, the authorship of the first five books of the Bible, also known as the Pentateuch, was ascribed to Moses. A significant reason for this is that the books themselves claim to have been written by Moses.[5] While some raised questions from time to time, these questions were widespread during the latter part of the nineteenth century, and many scholars began to doubt the Mosaic authorship. As a result, they set about developing a new theory for the Pentateuch's origin that came to be known as the Graf-Wellhausen or Documentary Hypothesis.

Basically, the Documentary Hypothesis states that the Pentateuch, rather than being the work of Moses, was the work of many different authors writing over about 500 years. The supporters of this theory find in the Pentateuch four major groups of authors, which they call strands. These strands are the J for Jehovah or Yahweh, E for Elohim, D for the Deuteronomic Code, and P for the Priestly tradition.

The oldest strands are the J and E, which are believed to date back in an oral form to about 800 to 900 B.C. They represent the religious traditions and beliefs of the Southern and Northern Kingdoms, respectively and scholars distinguish them by the different names they use for God. Scholars claim a third strand, the D, resulted from a religious revival around 650 B.C. Priests then wrote the fourth strand, the P, after the return of the Jews from 70 years of captivity in Babylon.

---

5   See Exodus 24:4 and Deuteronomy 31:9.

Scholars believe that around 500 B.C. to 400 B.C., these four strands were supposedly combined by editors into the five books that we now find in the Bible: Genesis, Exodus, Leviticus, Numbers, and Deuteronomy.

Today, the evidence for the Documentary Hypothesis consists of five main arguments. First, Deuteronomy 34 contains a description of Moses' death and burial. Since verse 6 states that "no man knows his burial place to this day," it would seem to have been written sometime after Moses had died. This verse raises an obvious question: How could Moses have written about his own death in terms of "to this day?"

A second argument concerns passages like Exodus 34:29, which refers to Moses in the third person (he) instead of the first person (I). The belief is that Moses would not have referred to himself as "he."

A third argument used by liberal scholars is that there are often parallel accounts of the same event. Sometimes these accounts seem to contradict each other, which would make a single author highly unlikely. An often-cited example is the creation accounts in the first two chapters of Genesis and how they differ in the order of creation. Chapter 1 has all of the animals created before Adam, while Chapter 2 claims that God created some animals after Adam. Which is it, and could one person have written both?

The fourth argument for multiple authors concerns the differences in style evident in the Pentateuch. Both the J and E strands have a storytelling approach, while the P strand reads like a legal document. The style of the D strand is smooth and flowing. These scholars claim different styles mean different writers.

The last main argument for multiple authors is that the different strands use different names for God. The J strand always uses the name Yahweh (YHWH)†[6] for God. On the other hand, the

---

6   YHWH (YaHWeH) was considered to be so holy that the Jews were reluctant to even pronounce it. During public readings, they would say 'aDoNaY (Lord) in it place. The Masoretes continues this tradition by writing the vowels of 'aDoNaY under YHWH. Many modern

E strand uses the name Elohim throughout Genesis and the first part of Exodus. In Exodus 6:3, the name of Yahweh is revealed to Moses, after which the E strand also uses this name.

The fact that the J strand uses Yahweh throughout the book of Genesis when E says that God first revealed this name to Moses is cited as further evidence against a single author.

The evidence for the Documentary Hypothesis can be summarized as follows:

- ✁ Moses' death is recorded.
- ✁ Moses is referred to in the third person.
- ✁ Parallel accounts that are contradictory.
- ✁ Use of different styles.
- ✁ Use of different names for God.

The general attitude of the time when scholars devised the theory was also crucial in its initial acceptance. It was the age of reason and scientific advancement, and evolution had recently ascended to the throne of biology. Everything was systematized and categorized. Many saw traditional religion as just another part of the irrational past that didn't fit into the new worldview.

This new worldview placed man as the master of his environment and Lord over creation. Many rejected the idea that in the past, some god told people how to live and what to believe. It was unthinkable that people needed to accept these beliefs.

Since everything else seemed to evolve, then why not religion? So scholars developed a new theory of religion. Religions, like life, started in primitive forms, in this case, polytheism. They then evolved into higher forms over time, culminating in monotheism. The Scottish Professor James Orr wrote the following in 1905 concerning the rejection of the Mosaic authorship:

---

translations also carry on this tradition. In the New International Version YHWH is translated as LORD (all caps) to distinguish it from lord. During the Renaissance scholars, mistakenly thought this combination of YHWH with the vowels for *'aDoNaY* should read as Jehovah (In German YHWH is JHVH).

> First, and perhaps deepest, of the reasons for this
> rejection is the a priori one, that such a conception of
> God as the Hebrew Scripture attributes to the patriarchs
> and to Moses was *impossible* for them at that stage of
> history. It is too elevated and spiritual for their minds to
> have entertained. The idea of the unity of God has for its
> correlates the ideas of the world and of humanity, and
> neither of these ideas, it is asserted, was possessed by
> ancient Israel.[7]5

When the Documentary Hypothesis appeared, it fits perfectly into this new worldview. It had the Books of Moses and the Jewish religion, not being given by God on Mt. Sinai but evolving from men for hundreds of years.

Also, as we have mentioned, there seemed to be significant conflicts between science and the Bible. For example, when scholars proposed the Documentary Hypothesis, they believed writing was unknown in Israel during the lifetime of Moses. Hermann Schultz, professor of Theology at the University of Gottingen, wrote in 1898 that,

> Of the legendary character of the pre-Mosaic nar-
> rators, the time of which they treat is a sufficient proof.
> It was a time before all knowledge of writing, a time sep-
> arated by an interval of more than four hundred years,
> of which there is absolutely no history. . . a time when
> in civilized countries writing was only beginning to be
> used. . . Even when writing had come into use, in the
> time, that is, between Moses and David, it would be but
> sparingly used, and much that happened to the people
> must still have been handed down simply as legend.[8]

If Moses did not know how to write, how could he have possibly written the Pentateuch?

During the later part of the nineteenth century and into the early part of the twentieth, it was challenging for conservative scholars to defend their position. The traditional views of the Bible conflicted with the new ideas provided by science. When put

---

7   James Orr, *The Problem of the Old Testament* (New York: Charles
     Scribner's Sons, 1906) p. 127.

8   Hermann Schultz, *Old Testament Theology* trans. from 4th ed. by H. A.
     Patterson (Edinburgh: T & T Clark, 1898) p. 25-26.

in terms of reason and science versus faith and religion, which it often was, many opted for reason and science.

The problem is, as we will see in later chapters, the conflicts between science and the Bible have largely disappeared. Today the evidence no longer supports rejecting Mosaic authorship.

For instance, it is now clear that religions do not move from polytheism to monotheism. If anything, the opposite is true. Gleason Archer, Professor of Old Testament at Trinity Evangelical Divinity School, has pointed out,

> It is an incontestable fact of history that no other nation (apart from those influenced by the Hebrew faith) ever did develop a true monotheistic religion which commanded the general allegiance of its people.[9]

The discovery of numerous examples of writing from Moses' time invalidated the argument that writing was unknown. Because of this, these two arguments are no longer used to support the Documentary Hypothesis. However, they did play an essential role in the original acceptance of the theory.

As for the arguments still used, they are questionable at best. Take, for example, the death of Moses at the end of the book of Deuteronomy (Deuteronomy 34:1-12). Although it is clear that Moses did not write this passage, this does not disprove his authorship of the rest of Deuteronomy or the other books in the Pentateuch. As Archer has pointed out,

> the closing chapter furnishes only that type of obituary which is often appended to the final work of great men of letters. An author's final work is often published posthumously (provided he has been writing up to the time of his death). Since Joshua is recorded to have been a faithful and zealous custodian of the Torah, Moses' literary achievement, it is quite unthinkable that he would have published it without appending such a notice of the decease of his great predecessor.[10]

---

9   Gleason Archer, *A Survey of Old Testament Introduction* (Chicago: Moody Press, 1974) p. 149.

10 Gleason Archer, *A Survey of Old Testament Introduction* (Chicago: Moody Press, 1974) p. 263.

A similar answer applies to the argument that the writer(s) of the Pentateuch refers to Moses in the third person and, therefore, could not have been Moses. Other authors used this practice in ancient times.

In his work, *Wars of the Jews*, Josephus referred to himself in the third person. Xenophon, a Greek historian and disciple of Socrates writing in the fifth century B.C., and Julius Caesar, whose account of the Gallic War in the first, both referred to themselves in the third person. No one questions the authorship of these books written in the third person. So why question the authorship of Moses for the same practice?

As for the supposed parallel accounts, conservative scholars have long since shown there is no reason to believe they exist. An illustration is the supposed differences in the creation stories in Genesis. Ancient writing did not follow the same practices and norms found in modern writing. They were not always chronological but, at times, followed other patterns. A writer could give a broad overview to put the subject in context and then go back and expand on the crucial details.[11] Genesis 2 is not a different view of creation by a second author, as claimed by supporters of the Documentary Hypothesis; it is a more detailed description of the creation. In chapter one of Genesis, Moses gives us a broad picture of the creation of the universe. In contrast, in chapter two, he gives us a detailed view of the creation of Adam and Eve.[12]

Regarding the different orders of creation, scholars have proposed two possibilities that would eliminate any contradiction. The first points to the meaning of the word translated as "formed" in the King James Version of Genesis 2:19. Supporters of this theory point out that this word can also mean "had formed." Thus,

---

11 Gleason Archer, *Encyclopedia of Bible Difficulties* (Grand Rapids: Zondervan, 1982) p. 68-9.

12 This is not an argument for a literal seven day creation, only that these two chapters form one coherent story and not two. One can accept that they form a single story and still reject the scientific validity of a literal seven day creation. The question of the scientific accuracy of this account will be discussed in Chapter 5.

the New International Version reads, "Now the LORD God had formed out of the ground all the beasts of the field and all the birds of the air." In other words, the animals brought before Adam were animals that God created earlier and now brought to Adam. He did not create them after Adam.

Others have suggested a different possibility. Genesis 2:19 only mentions the creation of two types of animals, "beast of the field" and "birds of the air." Yet, in the next verse, Adam names these and "livestock" as well. Elsewhere in the books of Moses, the writer always distinguishes livestock from beasts and birds.

As such, the writer does not include livestock among the "beast" and "birds" created for naming. God created the livestock earlier. According to this view, God did make all animals before man. When it was time for Adam to name the animals, the livestock were already close at hand, but many of the beasts and the birds were scattered across the earth. Therefore God created specimens of the beasts and birds for Adam to name.

In addition to these explanations, there are other reasons to question whether Genesis 1 and 2 actually form separate accounts of Creation.[13] Still, it should be clear that the claim that these are different accounts that demand separate authors is questionable.

The argument that there are different styles and thus different authors, fails to consider that the five books cover a wide range of topics, purposes, places, and times. Would one really expect a person to use the same style to record history (Genesis, Exodus), laws (Leviticus, Numbers), and speeches (Deuteronomy)? The different types we find in the Pentateuch reflect not many different authors but the wide variety of subject matters in these five books.

There is also the consideration of the possible use of scribes and their roles in shaping the style of a passage. The role and influ-

---

13 Others reasons would be the literary links between the chapters which would indicate they were a single literary unit and the absence of the creation of the earth, sun, moon, and heaven in the second account, which raises question whether it really can be considered a creation account.

ence of a scribe differed radically from person to person. A scribe might take dictation, capturing the writer's actual words. Or they might write the work for editing and proofing by the author. The more you move to the latter, the more influence a scribe would have over the style.

Finally, there is the issue of time. While Deuteronomy is generally accepted to have been written last, when the other books where written is not always clear. The timespan from the first to the last book could have been several decades, and a writers style can change.

The last significant argument still in use by those holding to the Documentary Hypothesis is that the different names for God found in the Pentateuch imply different authors. Yet, when we examine the names for God and their uses, it becomes pretty clear why the different names for God appear in the Bible. Multiple authors have nothing to do with it.

Each name has a special significance, and the author uses it only where appropriate. Elohim, as the general name for God, is used in Genesis 1 when God (Elohim) created the universe. YHWH (Yahweh), on the other hand, is the personal name for God and is used when God deals with his people, as in Genesis 2 when God (Yahweh) creates Adam and Eve.

Another problem with this argument is that it tends to be circular. Supporters claim that since the E strand uses the name Elohim while the J strand uses only YHWH, different authors wrote these strands. How can this claim be tested? Liberal scholars believe that later editors blended the various strands to form the first five books of the Bible. So how do they separate these strands from the existing text to test this claim? They use the names of God.

When Elohim appears in a passage, supporters of the Documentary Hypothesis assume that it is the work of the author of the E strand. When they see YHWH, the writer was the author of the J strand. So, of course, the E strand uses the name Elohim; that is how the E strand is determined to be the E strand. Because of this circular reasoning, the fact that the E strand uses the name Elohim does not support that there are different authors.

A version of this argument states that Exodus 6:3 says the name YHWH was unknown until Moses received it. Yet the name is used in Genesis, which records events before the time of Moses. How could it be used before it was known, again pointing to different authors? A better understanding of what YHWH means addresses this argument.

During Moses' time, names were more than just labels to distinguish one person from another. Names were to reveal something about the nature and character of a person. As a person changed, sometimes their name was changed, as when Abram (exalted father) became Abraham (father of many) in Genesis 17:1-8. The name YHWH was not given merely as a label the Jewish people could use when referring to God but as a description of God.

YHWH is the personal name for God and reflects a covenant with Him. While Abraham, Isaac, and Jacob knew of and used the name YHWH for God, they did not know God as YHWH. Their relationship to God was through the name El Shaddai – The Almighty God.

God told Moses that the relationship between Himself and His people would be different than it had been with Abraham, Isaac, and Jacob. God changed his relationship from God Almighty, the creator God, to the God of the Covenant, the God who keeps His promises. Since this was a matter of relationship and not just a name, Moses could not just tell everyone what God's name was. God needed to show them. He told Moses,

> Therefore, say to the Israelites: "I am the LORD, and I will bring you out from under the yoke of the Egyptians. I will free you from being slaves to them, and I will redeem you with an outstretched arm and with mighty acts of judgment. I will take you as my own people, and I will be your God. *Then you will know* that I am the LORD your God." (Exodus 6:6-7 Italics added)

SUPPORT FOR MOSAIC AUTHORSHIP

Each of the arguments used to support the Documentary Hypothesis fails to hold up under scrutiny. There is no substantial evidence to support it. But is there evidence in favor of the Mosaic authorship? The answer is yes! There is a large body of consistent internal evidence that does support the authorship by Moses.

Throughout the entire Bible, Moses is consistently referred to as the author of the Pentateuch. There are also the Jewish and Christian traditions, which both cite Moses as the author. Recent scholarship also supports the Mosaic authorship and argues against the Documentary Hypothesis.

Tradition holds that the book of Deuteronomy records the final speech Moses gave to the people of Israel before his death. The Documentary Hypothesis, on the other hand, holds that the book came out of a period of religious revival during the seventh century B.C.

Deuteronomy is in the form of a covenant between God and the Jewish people. Scholars know that covenants and treaties have specific structures and that these structures change over the years. Because of this, one way Deuteronomy can be dated is to compare it with other covenants and treaties. The structure of Deuteronomy should be similar to the structure of covenants and treaties written about the same time. The work of George Mendenhall and Meredith Kline shows a very close relationship between the book of Deuteronomy and ancient suzerainty treaties written by the Hittites.

Suzerainty treaties occur between a greater power and a lesser one, like a treaty between a king and a knight. The suzerainty treaties written by the Hittites during the fourteenth and thirteenth century B.C. do not resemble those written during the seventh and sixth century B.C. Since the structure of Deuteronomy corresponds to Hittite treaties, this is strong evidence that the book of Deuteronomy comes from the fourteenth or thirteenth century B.C., when Moses lived. It is also evidence against the claim it dates from the seventh or sixth century B.C., as supporters of the Documentary Hypothesis believe.[14]

Many other items point to a date for the Pentateuch earlier than that proposed by supporters of the Documentary Hypothesis. The detailed references to nomadic desert life, including sanitary instructions (Deuteronomy 23:12-13), show that the Pentateuch addresses a nation of wanderers, not farmers. The author demonstrates knowledge of Egypt and Sinai but not Canaan (Israel). The book describes some plants and animals, like the acacia tree and the ostrich, found in Egypt and Sinai but not in Canaan.[15] The reverse is never true, where the author describes animals peculiar to Canaan. When the author mentions Canaan, it is often in terms of Egypt or Sinai, places familiar to Moses and the Jewish people since they had just left (Genesis 13:10).

Archaism in the language also supports the Mosaic authorship. Many of the words, phrases and spellings used in the Pentateuch were common to the period in which Moses lived but were obsolete and not used when the Documentary Hypothesis claims the author wrote.[16]

For example, at the time of Moses, in Egypt, a Pharoah was simply Pharoah, without mention of his name. In later years, this switched and a Pharaoh was referred to by name, but without the title. Thus the usage in the Pentateuch fits the early time, not the later. Likewise, the pronoun she in these books uses the older spelling HW' rather than HY' found in later books. [17]

The Documentary Hypothesis probably would have been rejected if what is now known had been known. There is insufficient solid evidence to reject the Mosaic authorship and considerable

---

14 Gleason Archer, *Encyclopedia of Bible Difficulties* (Grand Rapids: Zondervan, 1982) p. 259-261.

15 Gleason Archer, *Encyclopedia of Bible Difficulties* (Grand Rapids: Zondervan, 1982) p. 119.

16 Gleason Archer, *Encyclopedia of Bible Difficulties* (Grand Rapids: Zondervan, 1982) p. 121.

17 Gleason Archer, *A Survey of Old Testament Introduction* (Chicago: Moody Press, 1974) p. 115-118.

evidence to support it. Yet, when scholars proposed the Documentary Hypothesis, much of this evidence was unknown. If this is true, why is the Documentary Hypothesis still accepted by liberal scholars and taught in most secular universities as a confirmed fact?

The main reason for the acceptance of the hypothesis today is that it became the norm at the turn of the 20th century. Since then, liberal scholars have based most of their research on the Hebrew Scripture on this hypothesis. The Documentary Hypothesis has become accepted and deeply ingrained into liberal thinking. To discard the hypothesis now would throw out much of liberal scholarship.

While the evidence may not be strong enough for it to be accepted were it proposed today, the Documentary Hypothesis has not been totally disproven and is still retained.

In many cases, proponents no longer defend the Documentary Hypothesis; they just present it. In some of the classes I took, the professors refused to discuss the subject. Rather than teach it himself, one professor had the students learn about the Documentary Hypothesis from an interactive computer program. This way, he did not have to spend class time discussing the matter.

Another professor refused to discuss any problems with the hypothesis. His attitude was if you did not accept it, you were not approaching the subject in a truly scientific manner.

Those who actively defend the Documentary Hypothesis do so not by pointing out its sound scholarly backing but by ridiculing the Bible. Instead of responding to the arguments of those accepting Mosaic authorship, they usually ignore any critic of the Documentary Hypothesis or write them off as religious fanatics who do not understand modern scholarship.

We can see this attitude in a book that received some media attention. Richard E. Friedman, in his book, *Who Wrote the Bible?*, presents a case for a modified version of the Documentary Hypothesis. While Friedman spends a lot of time dealing with the differing views of the Documentary Hypothesis and explaining why his understanding of the hypothesis is correct, he completely ignores those arguments put forth by conservative scholars. To read his book, you would think that the term "conservative scholar" was contradictory. Friedman states as much when he writes,

> At present, however, there is hardly a biblical schol-ar in the world actively working on the problem who would claim that the Five Books of Moses were writ-ten by Moses – or by any one person. Scholars argue about the number of different authors who wrote any given biblical book... They express varying degrees of satisfaction or dissatisfaction with the usefulness of the hypothesis for literary or historical purposes. But the hypothesis itself continues to be the starting point of research, no serious student of the Bible can fail to study it, and no other explanation of the evidence has come close to challenging it.[18]

If this were not enough, Friedman goes on to add in the ac-companying footnote,

> There are many persons who claim to be biblical scholars. I refer to scholars who have the necessary training in languages, biblical archaeology, and literary and historical skills to work on the problem, and who meet, discuss, and debate their ideas and research with other scholars through scholarly journals, conferences, and etc.[19]

While Friedman's statements may sound impressive, they are nevertheless false. Yet, the fact that he makes such erroneous statements is not all that surprising. Among liberal scholars, the debate concerning the Documentary Hypothesis is over. They have declared victory for themselves, and no longer feel any need to present both sides of the issue. While conservative scholars have addressed the tenets of the Documentary Hypothesis, those trained at schools supporting the Hypothesis often have not been exposed to any opposing arguments. Based on their learning, no real opposition exists.

---

18 Richard E Friedman, *Who Wrote the Bible?* (New York: Summit Books, 1987) p. 28.
19 Richard E Friedman, *Who Wrote the Bible?* (New York: Summit Books, 1987) p. 261.

Gleason Archer, one of those supposedly nonexistent conservative scholars, pointed this out in a review he wrote of Friedman's book. In that review, Archer wrote the following concerning these statements by Friedman,

> The Author of this book is a typical product of the Liberalism of the nineteenth century, brought up on Wellhausen's Documentary Hypothesis, and carefully screened from acquaintance with any type of scholarship that disagrees with the so-called "settled results of modern scholarship." Not a single conservative scholar is mentioned in the entire book, and he seems to be totally unaware that any educated thinker could disagree with the Liberal Establishment.[20]

As for Friedman's contention that there are no scholars who would accept the traditional position on the Mosaic authorship, Archer writes,

> True scholarship is thus restricted to those who screen themselves off from all contrary evidence and dogmatically content themselves with repeating arguments long since refuted by well informed and superbly trained products of the foremost universities in America... The fact is that there are Old Testament specialists who have been trained in schools like Harvard and Princeton and Chicago University, who have received earned doctorates, who have become skilled in all of the relevant languages and archeological discoveries, who have attended and participated in all of the leading scholarly conventions, and who have authored texts that are studied by college and seminary students all over the world, who still adhere to the Mosaic authorship of the Pentateuch.[21]

The belief that all real scholars accept liberal views concerning the Bible carries over from the works of liberal scholars and appears as a fact in many popular writings. Isaac Asimov, in *Asimov's Guide to the Bible*, wrote the following concerning the question of a possible second Isaiah,

---

20   Gleason Archer, *A Summary Critique a Review of Who Wrote the Bible? by Richard Friedman, Christian Research Journal*, Vol. 10 No 2 Fall 87 p. 25.

21   Gleason Archer, *A Summary Critique a Review of Who Wrote the Bible? by Richard Friedman Christian Research Journal*, Vol. 10 No 2 Fall 87 p. 25.

> It is possible to argue, if one is wedded to the literal
> word of the Bible, that the Isaiah of Hezekiah's time fore-
> saw the period of the Exile in great detail, down to the
> name and deeds of the monarch who was to establish
> the Persian Empire and liberate the Jews, and that he
> spoke his vision in a style that was altered from what it
> had been. This point of view, however, has no important
> advocates today.[22]

Unless Asimov defines "*important advocates*" as only those who believe that there were two Isaiahs, his last statement is simply wrong. Many conservative scholars accept the unity of the book of Isaiah. As with the arguments for the Documentary Hypothesis, the arguments for a second Isaiah are questionable, while there is strong evidence for accepting a single author.[23]

Asimov's statement also reveals a primary reason for the continued acceptance of liberal views concerning the Bible. For Isaiah to have written about the Exile in such detail, he must have known about the future. If you reject that predictive prophecy is possible, then you will not believe that Isaiah wrote those sections of the book that predict the future. In many cases, accepting traditional views requires the acceptance of prophecy and the supernatural.

Because of this, no matter how strong the evidence put forth by conservatives, it will not be strong enough to overcome the bias of liberal scholars against the supernatural. So even though the evidence favors the Mosaic authorship of the first five books of the Bible, we are not likely to see the Documentary Hypothesis disappear any time soon.

THE NEW TESTAMENT

When we look at the New Testament, we find a very similar situation. Liberal scholars, applying theories developed during the nineteenth century, try to date much of the New Testament very

---

22 Isaac Asimov, *Asimov's Guide to the Bible - Volume I, The Old Testament* (Garden City, New York: Doubleday, 1968) p. 549.

23 For evidence which supports the unity of Isaiah see:
Geoffrey W. Grogan, *Isaiah The Expositor's Bible Commentary* ed. Frank E Gaebelein (Grand Rapids, MI: Regency, 1986) p. 6-11.

late and dispute the authorship of many books. However, we do not find the same consensus among liberal scholars regarding the New Testament as we do with the Hebrew Scripture. In *An Introduction to New Testament Literature*, Donald Juel, James Ackerman, and Thayer Warshaw question the traditional view of authorship for all four of the Gospels.[24]   On the other hand, Elwyn Tilden of Lafayette College, although he rejects Matthew as the author of the Gospel of Matthew, sees support for Mark and Luke as the authors of their Gospels.[25]

Scholarly criticism of the New Testament is a complex field of study, and there are many ways to approach it. Our approach divides it into two main categories: historical criticism and literary criticism, each having different schools of thought. As the name implies, historical criticism critically examines a book's historical context and setting. Literary criticism is the critical evaluation of a book's literary content dealing with issues such as authorship and the nature of possible sources.

HISTORICAL CRITICISM

Few scholars, whether liberal or conservative, would dispute the need to examine the contents of the New Testament critically. Most would argue that adequately understanding a book requires understanding the historical situation. What divides liberal and conservative scholars is the question of how the writers of the New Testament used history. Did they accurately describe the historical settings of events, or did they distort it to fit their particular theological points?

Among liberal scholars, there are two main views. One view, typified by the writings of the German theologian Rudolf Bult-

---

24 Donald Juel, James Ackerman and Thayer Warshaw, *An Introduction to New Testament Literature* (Nashville: Abingdon, 1978).

25 Elwyn E Tilden, *Introduction for the Gospels of Matthew, Mark, and Luke.* in *The New Oxford Annotated Bible with the Apocrypha* ed. Herbert G May and Bruce M Metzger (New York: Oxford University Press, 1977) Matthew - p. 1171, Mark - p. 1213, Luke - p. 1240.

mann, holds that the authors' faith so distorts any history within the New Testament that it is impossible to extract it. In other words, the text of the New Testament is of no historical value whatsoever. The New Testament can tell us nothing about the historical Jesus. It only tells us what the early church believed about Him. According to Martin Dibelius,

> The first Christians had no interest in reporting the life and passion of Jesus objectively to mankind, sine ira et studio. They wanted nothing else than to win as many as possible to salvation in the last hour just before the end of the world, which they believed to be at hand. Those early Christians were not interested in history.[26]

The problem with this approach is that it assumes the New Testament writers did not care about history. These scholars reject the history recorded in the New Testament unless supported by other documentation. The question is: If the writers of the New Testament were not concerned with history, then why did they get the details of the historical setting correct?

As we shall see in the next chapter, archaeological discoveries have confirmed many details recorded in the New Testament. Many of these details have no theological significance and only provide historical background, yet they are still accurately described.

In the book of Acts, Luke uses the term "*first man*" as the title of the leader of the island of Malta. Even though this was an unusual title for a leader, it was the proper title to use in this instance. Why would Luke go to the trouble of using the unusual, though proper term, if accuracy was of no importance to him?

The second significant view of history taken by liberal scholars is *Religionsgeschichte,* or the history-of-religions approach. This approach views the New Testament as a collection of books influenced by several external movements, such as Greek philosophy and Gnosticism. Here the scholar's task is to distinguish and separate these external influences so they can reveal the "true" history.

---

26   Martin Dibelius, *Gospel Criticism and Christology* (London: Ivor Nicholson and Watson Ltd., 1935) p. 16.

This view depends on a theory of religion, holding that religions are the product of the environment in which they exist. Accordingly, Christianity, rather than given by God through divine revelation, was created by modifying the views and beliefs existing in and around first-century Israel and then applying them to fit a Jewish worldview.

Liberal scholars attempt to support this view by pointing to concepts in the New Testament, which also exist in other movements of the time. These parallels, they claim, demonstrate a link between the two. The problem is that these scholars based these parallels on documents written long after the New Testament.

For instance, some liberal scholars believe that some books of the New Testament show a gnostic influence in their teachings. Still, very little evidence supports the notion that Gnosticism reached a high enough point of development that Christianity could have borrowed from it until after the New Testament's completion.[27] It is far more likely that Gnosticism borrowed from Christianity than Christianity from Gnosticism.

Conservatives also have two views of history regarding the New Testament. The smaller of the two groups believes that the historical setting of the New Testament plays an insignificant role in our understanding of the Bible. The other group agrees with liberal scholars that the historical setting of the New Testament is essential. Still, they disagree with many of the conclusions that liberal scholars have reached.

What separates liberal scholars from conservatives is similar to what separates an optimist from a pessimist: point of view. Is the glass half empty or half full? Even though recent archaeological discoveries have borne out the reliability of the New Testament in many places, many liberal scholars still retain their skepticism. Donald Guthrie succinctly summarizes the situation as follows,

---

27 Donald Guthrie, *The Historical and Literary Criticism of the New Testament* in *The Expositor's Bible Commentary* ed. Frank E Gaebelein (Grand Rapids, MI: Zondervan, 1979) p. 443.

> The real crux is the point of departure in the critical quest. Destructive criticism begins with the assumption that nothing is valid until proved true, which a priori rules out the possibility of treating such a basic Christian event as the resurrection of Jesus as historical. Constructive criticism takes the opposite view and regards as valid the claims of the NT [New Testament] until they can be proved false... Much of the difference of opinion between conservative schools of thought and the more liberal ones arises from the presuppositions from which they assess historical validity.[28]

In the final analysis, your view of historical criticism will depend mainly on how you view the reliability of the New Testament. As we will see in chapter six, the Bible is historically reliable.

LITERARY CRITICISM

The differences among scholars in Historical Criticism lead to even more significant differences in Literary Criticism because the two fields of study are closely interrelated. How you view the historical accuracy of the New Testament will strongly influence your view of how the books came to exist. For example, suppose you do not accept that the Gospels are historically accurate. In that case, you are unlikely to accept their claim to have been written by eyewitnesses (John 19:35, 1 John 1:1, 2 Peter 1:16).

One of the most significant areas of study in the literary criticism of the New Testament is trying to solve what has come to be called the Synoptic Problem. The Synoptic Problem seeks an understanding of the relationship between the Gospels of Matthew, Mark, and Luke.

Even a casual reading of the Gospels reveals that the first three, known as the Synoptic Gospels, are remarkably similar. At the same time, the Gospel of John differs significantly in its structure from the other three.

---

28 Donald Guthrie, *The Historical and Literary Criticism of the New Testament* in *The Expositor's Bible Commentary* ed. Frank E Gaebelein (Grand Rapids, MI: Zondervan, 1979) p. 443.

The first three Gospel accounts are the same in many places, almost word for word. In other places, only two of the Gospels are similar, Matthew paralleling Mark or Luke paralleling Mark. Sometimes Matthew and Luke are similar in wording, while Mark is not.

The similarity in the outline and wording of passages among the Synoptic Gospels has led most scholars, both liberal and conservative, to conclude that these three Gospels are related to one another in some fashion. The exact nature of this relationship is unclear. It is trying to understand this relationship which is the Synoptic Problem.

One writer using another as a source when writing a Gospel, in and of itself, does not pose a problem for conservatives. Luke acknowledges other accounts at the start of his Gospel. He says he based his on the results of careful investigation (Luke 1:1-4).

Also, the differences between the Gospel accounts do not represent any error or contradiction, as some have tried to claim.[29] Instead, the differences are in the words chosen when describing an event, the selection and ordering of events, and the details mentioned.

For many scholars, the Synoptic Problem is well on its way to a solution if one assumes Mark was first and Matthew and Luke used Mark when writing their Gospels. For support, scholars point out that most of the material found in Mark is repeated in Matthew and/or Luke. If Matthew or Luke differ from Mark in the ordering of certain events, the other will agree with Mark at that point. Nowhere do we find Matthew and Luke agreeing with each other in the sequence of events without also agreeing with Mark.

While this theory helps explain much of the Synoptic Problem, it does have some problems of its own. For one, it goes against the testimony of some early church fathers who believed Matthew

---

29 We will examine the question of contradictions in the Bible in chapter
    six.

was the first Gospel.[30] Concerning the ordering of events, this is not as conclusive as it may seem. Mark could just as easily have worked from Matthew and Luke, agreeing with them when they agreed and then choosing to follow one or the other when they differed.

In fact, an alternative theory by J.J. Griesbach builds on the unique relationship between Mark and Luke and Matthew to claim that Mark was the last of the three, not the first. This theory notes that Mark begins at the point Matthew and Luke first deal with similar material and ends at the point they diverge for the last time.

In between, Mark always follows either Luke or Matthew. More importantly, when Mark changes from following one of the Gospels, he never backtracks. It is as if the author had the scrolls of both Matthew and Luke before him. He follows one for a while and then the other. This pattern would indicate that either Mark was last or that the writers of Matthew and Luke agreed upon which sections of Mark they would use. Matthew would follow one section, Luke the next. Yet such coordination is highly unlikely.

This pattern of use between the three Gospels conforms well with early accounts that place Matthew as the first Gospel. The early church fathers believed Mark's Gospel resulted from a series of lectures given by Peter, transcribed by Mark, and it is not hard to picture Peter preaching alternatively from Matthew and Luke, adding his personal reminisces to their accounts.

Interestingly in this light, while Mark is the shortest Gospel, the individual accounts in Mark tend to be longer and are full of personal details.[31] It is as if Peter is stitching the Gospels of Matthew and Luke together to show that they are one.

There are historical reasons why Peter would have felt this was necessary. The internal evidence shows that Matthew wrote

---

30 Donald Guthrie, *New Testament Introduction, 3rd ed.* (Downers Grove, Ill: InterVarsity, 1970) pp. 33-38.

31 That Mark is the shortest is often cited as one of the reasons that Mark was written first, as there is a tendency for later writers to expand on the works they use as their sources. But given that Mark's individual accounts are longer this argument actually argues in favor of Mark being written last.

his Gospel for a Jewish audience who understood Jewish customs and practices. Luke, on the other hand, was written for Gentiles. Given the tensions between these groups, it would have been easy for some to mistake Luke's Gospel for a new and different Gospel rather than the same Gospel presented in a way Gentiles could more easily understand.

In this light, Peter gave his sermons to bridge this gap and unite the Gospels and the church. This understanding would also explain Mark's traditional placement between Matthew and Luke.

Still, seeing Mark as first or last does not answer all the problems. There are places where Matthew and Luke are very similar to one another and yet different from Mark.

Up to this point, the liberal and conservative scholars are pretty much in agreement, or at least one can find both types of scholars taking various positions on this question. As a further solution to the Synoptic Problem, liberal scholars have proposed the existence of an unknown source referred to as "Q," *quelle* being the word for source in German.

This theory has been expanded even further into a four-source theory among some American and British scholars. While conservative scholars have no problem with sources in and of themselves, these liberal theories parallel the Documentary Hypothesis. They reduced the writers of the Gospels to mere editors who gathered and organized the work of others.

The main problem with these additional sources is that they entirely lack any external evidence to support them. No copies or fragments of the supposed Q document have ever been found. Researchers can find no mention in any writings of the period of anything that could be the Q document.

So far, the Q document remains a creation of the scholarly mind. Considering the large number of New Testament manuscripts, it seems unlikely that such an important document would have entirely disappeared without a trace.[32]

---

32   In light of this, some scholars have proposed that the Q source was not a
     written document at all, and instead consisted of the teachings that the

Donald Guthrie of the University of London summarizes the results of Literary criticism in this area as follows,

> Though the Mark-Q hypothesis exercised a profound influence on the critical approach to the synoptic Gospels in the nineteenth and early twentieth centuries, more recently the Q hypothesis itself has come under increasing criticism. Also the view that Luke used Matthew has gained support. This latter view goes a long way toward dispensing with Q. Even the theory of Mark's priority has not gone unchallenged, though most NT scholars retain it for want of a better alternative. All in all, the changing fortunes of source criticism show that literary criticism has not achieved and cannot achieve conclusive results in the examination of the origins of the Gospels.[33]

ON SHAKY GROUND

As we have seen, these theories rest on shaky ground and remain unproven. Still, they are used, along with a general skepticism of the historical content of the New Testament and the modern theories on the development of religion, to arrive at late dates for many books of the New Testament. They form the basis for rejecting the traditional views concerning the authorship of the New Testament.

The reliance on presuppositions and unverified theories has often led liberal scholars to conclusions later contradicted by archeological finds. A classic example of this concerns the dating of the Gospel of John.

Due to the differences in the structure of John's Gospel compared to Matthew, Mark, and Luke, and its highly developed theology, many liberal scholars in the nineteenth century argued the date for the Gospel of John must be very late. William Sanday, writing about the liberal scholar Dr. O. Pfleiderer's view of the Gospel of John, stated that,

> For him the Gospel is from first to last a didactic work in the guise of history; it is a "transparent allegory of religious and dogmatic ideas." He would place

---

disciples committed to memory during or shortly after Jesus' ministry.

33 Donald Guthrie, *New Testament Introduction, 3rd ed.* (Downers Grove, Ill: InterVarsity, 1970) pp. 443.

> the first draft of the Gospel about the year 135, the last
> chapter and the First Epistle about 150.[34]

John A. T. Robinson, in his book *Redating The New Testament,* summarized the history of the dating of the Gospel of John as follows,

> The story of the dating of the fourth Gospel in
> modern scholarship is an extraordinarily simple one.
> On the one hand, the conservatives have not had occa-
> sion (at any rate until very recently) to shift their position
> and have consistently put the gospel in or about the
> last decade of the first century. On the other hand, the
> radical critics like Baur began by dating it anything up
> to 170 and have since steadily come down. Thus P. W.
> Schmiedel, who wrote the article on John, Son of Zebe-
> dee, in the Encyclopedia Biblica, occupied a mediating
> position with a date between 132 and 140.[35]

Of course, a date for the Gospel of John in the middle of the second century A.D. would preclude the apostle John from being the author. A date this late would mean that the Gospel was composed after John's death.

This belief in a late date for John's Gospel existed among liberal scholars until a fragment of John's Gospel was discovered dating between A.D. 125 and A.D. 130. This manuscript was made up to 50 years before the liberal scholars dated John's Gospel!

This fragment was discovered in Egypt. Allowing for the average time required for the copying and transmission, the date of authorship would have been no later than A.D. 100, the traditional date for the Gospel. Because of this fragment, liberal and conservative scholars generally accept A.D. 90-100 as the date for the Gospel of John.[36]

Conservative scholars do not object to scholarly criticism applied to the Bible. It is the way it is applied and the presuppositions

---

34 William Sanday, *The Criticism of the Fourth Gospel* (New York: Charles Scribner's Sons, 1921) p. 26.

35 John A T Robinson, *Redating The New Testament* (London: SCM Press LTD, 1976) p. 259.

36 Recently some scholars have argued for an even earlier date, possibly as early as A.D. 50-60.

used. Liberal criticism, rather than being a constructive force, destructively attempts to dismantle the Bible to fit the current thinking on the development of religion.

The Jesus Seminar mentioned at the beginning of this chapter is an example of this type of scholarship. The scholars of the Jesus Seminar concluded that Jesus did not say, among other things, the Lord's Prayer. Charles Hedrick, one of the scholars at the meeting, stated concerning the Lord's Prayer that it,

> was the kind of prayer that would have been need-
> ed in a community which had a formal liturgy, a formal
> worship.[37]

In other words, the Lord's Prayer was too formal to have been spoken by Jesus. Since, according to liberal belief, Christ did not know He was starting a new religion, He would not have given us such a formal prayer. What is the hard evidence for this conclusion? There is none. Like the other liberal conclusion we have looked at, it is mainly based on the assumptions of liberal scholars and their theories concerning the development of religion.

Who do they think wrote the Lord's Prayer? The general consensus of the scholars at the meeting was that the writer of the Q document also composed the Lord's Prayer. Of course, to accept this, one must first accept that there was a Q document, which, as we have seen, is questionable. On the other hand, given the lack of evidence for such a writer, there is little to conflict with the theory that whoever wrote Q also wrote the Lord's prayer.

For the sake of argument, let's say these scholars are correct in their conclusion that the Lord's Prayer is not a personal prayer. Would it really be unreasonable to believe that Jesus, who is God incarnate, would have known the outcome of His actions? Indeed, as the Son of God, Christ knew that a world religion would emerge after His death and resurrection. Is it really that difficult to believe that He could have given a prayer for such a setting?

---

37 Quoted by John Dart, *Bible Scholars Say Jesus Didn't Create or Teach Lord's Prayer, Los Angles Times*, Oct. 18, 1988, Part I p. 3.

So the main reason for rejecting the Lord's Prayer does not hold up. The real problem is the Bible, as it exists, does not conform to the liberal theories concerning religion. What the Jesus Seminar has done, rather than change their theories to fit the evidence, is change the Bible to fit their theories.

CONCLUSION

We have seen that the contention that modern scholarship has shown the Bible to be unreliable is questionable. While some scholars make bold statements concerning the Bible, such as Jesus did not say the Lord's Prayer, these statements are somewhat like the Wizard of Oz. They sound impressive only until you pull back the curtain and examine their reasoning. When we do this, we find the results no longer seem quite so sound.

If you accept the presuppositions upon which liberals base their scholarship and ignore the objections, the results will seem reasonable and justified. But if you reject these presuppositions, as do conservative scholars, the results will seem questionable if not outright wrong.

The main problem with liberalism is that it exalts rationalism above God and the Bible. The question is often asked: Why shouldn't the Bible be subject to reason? The problem is not with reason but with the worldview in which you apply reason. Reason and rationalism are not the same things. Rationalism is not just a tool to be applied to the Bible. It is, in many ways, a competing worldview that rejects any supernatural influence in nature.

This rejection of supernatural influences forms the basis for the modern critical approach to the Bible. As James Orr wrote at the beginning of the twentieth century,

> to a large and influential school of critical inquirers
> – Those, moreover, who have had the most to do with
> the shaping of the current critical theories – this question of a supernatural origin for the religion of Israel is

already foreclosed; is ruled out at the start as a priori inadmissible.[38]

If you reject any supernatural influence in nature, then it is impossible to maintain the reliability of the Bible. Without supernatural influences, you must discount the Gospels saying that Jesus did miracles. If Jesus did not do miracles, the accounts that describe them must be in error. If the accounts are in error, those who wrote them were not well acquainted with the ministry of Jesus, or if they were, they lied. Either way, what they have written is unreliable. Therefore the Bible is unreliable.

As before, we reached this conclusion without considering any actual evidence for the reliability of the text. The presupposition and the fact that the Bible says Jesus did miracles is all it took. The conclusion follows from the presuppositions, in this case, the a priori rejection of the supernatural.

When liberal scholars that reject the possibility of supernatural influence conclude that the Bible is unreliable, is it any wonder their conclusions are not accepted by those who do not make the same assumptions?

When we examine the Old and New Testaments critically, unless we rule out the possibility of supernatural influences from the start,[39] the evidence is quite strong for the traditional view concerning dates and authorship.[40] The physical evidence discovered

---

38 James Orr, *The Problem of the Old Testament* (New York: Charles Scribner's Sons, 1906) p. 12.

39 This is not saying scholars must accept the supernatural nature of the Bible at the start. This would be just as much a leap of faith as the liberal scholars' rejection of it. One need only leave open the possibility and then let the evidence decide the matter.

40 For detailed examinations of the evidence for the traditional dates and authorship of the book of the Bible see:
For the books of the Old Testament:
Gleason L Archer Jr., *A Survey of Old Testament Introduction* (Chicago: Moody Press, 1994.)
For the books of the New Testament:
Donald Guthrie, *New Testament Introduction, 3rd ed.* (Downers Grove, Ill: InterVarsity, 1970).

through such endeavors as archaeology also supports traditional views.

This evidence has been a limiting factor for liberal scholars. It has tended to move them back towards, and in some cases to, the positions held by conservatives. Some questions remain for scholarship, such as the relationship of the Synoptic Gospels. Still, these questions are mainly of concern only to scholars. They in no way threaten the Christian understanding of the Bible as the Word of God.

Carson, Moo, and Morris, *An Introduction to the New Testament* (Grand Rapids, MI: Zondervan, 1992).

3

THE BIBLE AND ARCHAEOLOGY

The remarkable recovery of the past through recent archaeology has revolutionized the writing of ancient history which once was totally dependent upon what biblical and classical writers had said. The new increment to the knowledge of the past has demanded a reassessment of the older sources and evoked widely differing opinions.
James B. Pritchard [1]

ARCHAEOLOGY IS NEVER THE ADVENTUROUS and exciting quest for treasure that you sometimes see depicted in movies. Instead, it is a slow, methodical search for knowledge. Archaeologists often do not realize the importance of discoveries at the site of a dig but later in the laboratory.

In 1975, archaeologists digging around Jerusalem discovered two small silver scrolls. After a preliminary examination, they cataloged the scrolls and stored them for future research. There they remained for eleven years.

In 1986, researchers finally got around to a more extensive examination of the scrolls. Slowly and carefully, the scrolls were unrolled and examined under a microscope. To their surprise, the researchers found the scrolls contained a priestly blessing from the book of Numbers that was "identical in almost every feature to the later version that is used today."[2]

---

1   James B. Pritchard, in forward to Magnus Magnusson, *Archaeology of the Bible.*

2   *A Startling Revelation About the Good Book* Discover, 7:10-11 Aug. 1986.

The most exciting thing about these scrolls is that they date from the beginning of the sixth century B.C., hundreds of years before the oldest text previously known! Thus "with the discovery and deciphering of two tiny silver scrolls, biblical history will have to change."[3]

What made these scrolls so revolutionary is that the beginning of the sixth century B.C. was fifty years before the exile of the Jews into Babylon. As we saw in the last chapter, according to the Documentary Hypothesis, the dating for the book of Numbers is after the exile. These scrolls contained a quote from a book 120 years too early. While from the liberal view, something was wrong, this discovery only helps to confirm the traditional view that Moses wrote the book of Numbers.

Many critics would have us believe that the Bible contains nothing but myths and legends. When asked how agnostics regard the Bible, the noted philosopher and agnostic Bertrand Russell stated,

> He does not think that it is divinely inspired; he thinks its early history legendary, and no more exactly true than that in Homer.[4]

During the nineteenth century, the general consensus among liberal scholars was that you could believe very few (if any) accounts in the Bible. Julius Wellhausen, who was one of the leading developers of the Documentary Hypothesis, wrote in 1878 that from the Bible,

> we attain to no historical knowledge of the patriarchs, but only of the time when the stories about them arose in the Israelite people.[5]

Hermann Schultz wrote the following concerning the biblical account,

---

3   *A Startling Revelation About the Good Book* Discover, 7:10-11 Aug. 1986.
4   Bertrand Russell, *What is an Agnostic Religions of America*, ed. Leo Rosten (New York: Simon and Schuster, 1975) pp. 287-8.
5   Julius Wellhausen, *Prolegomena to the History of Israel* Trans. Black and Menzies (New York: World Publishing, 1957) pp. 318-19.

> Genesis is the book of sacred legend, with a myth-
> ical introduction... From Abraham to Moses we have
> national legend pure and simple, mixed with a variety
> of mythical elements which have become almost un-
> recognizable.[6]

As archaeology has expanded our knowledge of biblical times, those who were the most skeptical needed to rethink their positions, not those who have held traditional views. Even liberal scholars have recognized this change.

Samuel Sandmel, a professor at the University of Chicago Divinity School, although rejecting a traditional approach to the Bible, nevertheless acknowledges the support modern archaeology has given to the biblical accounts,

> Nineteenth-century biblical scholars, especially
> those influenced by the Graf-Wellhausen hypothesis,
> tended to be suspicious of the direct statements of
> Scripture; to oversimplify, they considered most doc-
> uments late, and all of them extravagantly and falsely
> glorifying the past. Archaeology has refuted such skep-
> tical scholars.[7]

So just how reliable is the Bible? Does archaeology prove the Bible is correct? The simple answer is no.

PROOF OR SUPPORT?

While archaeology can provide us with a general picture of life during a specific period, it cannot be expected to confirm the individual details. As G. K. Chesterton wrote,

> How could physical science prove that man is not
> depraved? You do not cut a man open to find sins. You
> do not boil him until he gives forth the unmistakable
> green fumes of depravity. How could physical science
> find any traces of a moral fall? What traces did the writer
> expect to find? Did he expect to find a fossil Eve with a
> fossil apple inside her? Did he suppose that the ages

---

6   Hermann Schultz, *Old Testament Theology* Trans. from 4th ed. by H. A,. Patterson (Edinburgh: T & T Clark, 1898) p. 31.

7   Samuel Sandmel, *The Hebrew Scriptures, an Introduction to Their Literature and Religious Ideas* (New York: Oxford University Press, 1978) p. 515.

would have spared for him a complete skeleton of Adam
attached to a slightly faded fig-leaf?[8]

What, then, can we expect from archaeology? For the most part, we can only look to archaeology to tell us some general information about the period during which the events described in the Bible took place. We might, for example, expect archaeology to give us some background on slavery during the eighteenth century B.C. and then check whether or not this conforms to what the Bible describes. We could not reasonably expect archaeologists to discover a bill of sale to prove Joseph was indeed sold into slavery by his brothers.

When we find that the general details of a certain period, as revealed by archaeology, agree with the descriptions in the Bible, does this constitute proof that the Bible is correct? This conclusion would depend on what one considers proof.

While in a few areas like math, where proof is clearly defined, in most areas, proof is a very ill-defined concept and is somewhat subjective.[9] Even in areas with some definition, such as a court of law, it still varies. In a criminal case, for example, the standard of evidence that constitutes proof is beyond a reasonable doubt. In a civil case, on the other hand, the standard of proof is the much lower standard of preponderance of the evidence. Ultimately, proof is simply the level of evidence required to conclude something is true.

Since the level of evidence required to conclude that something is true varies from situation to situation and from person to person, when someone says, "prove it," what they are asking is not always clear. For some, this is an honest request for evidence. For others, however, this is more of a defense mechanism since anything can be rejected simply by raising the standard of proof just a little bit higher than the available evidence.

---

8   G. K. Chesterton, *All Things Considered.* (New York: John Lane, 1913) pp. 189-90.

9   For a more complete discussion of the proof, evidence and what is true, see Elgin Hushbeck, *Seeking Truth: How to Move From Partisan Bickering to Building Consensus* (Gonzalez, Florida: Energion, 2022).

While whether the evidence from archaeology constitutes some proof is somewhat murky, it is clear that it does lend a great deal of credence to the biblical accounts. A significant reason for this support is times and customs change. Liberal scholars claim that much of the Bible was written long after the described events, assuming they occurred at all. If true, these events would have been described in terms of the customs and conventions familiar to the time of their writing, not when they occurred.

This is a very common phenomenon. While today we expect a high level of accuracy when we, for example, see historical events in movies, this is a somewhat recent development. Throughout much of human history, people had little understanding of the past. Writers and artists depicted events using the day's standards and customs.

You can see a humorous example of this in *Back to the Future III* when Doc Brown gets a cowboy outfit for Marty so he will fit in when he goes back in time. While, the outfit was in line with what Doc Brown saw in the movies, Marty's outfit did not match the period.

You can also see this in many paintings of biblical events during the Middle Ages and Renaissance. In these paintings, the background details, such as the types of buildings, style of clothes, etc., represent the time the artists were painting and not the biblical era they depict. Thus many of these paintings show Joseph and Mary dressed in clothes more typical of thirteenth-century Italy than first-century Israel.

If the stories in the Bible are later inventions or exaggerations, then we would expect the background details to represent the period in which they were written. This would especially be true if hundreds of years had passed, and people had forgotten the customs of the earlier period. When archaeology confirms the background details of a biblical account, it strongly supports it as having been written close to the time of the events.

A QUESTION OF DATES

One problem with the evidence provided by archaeology is that the dates are still uncertain for many of the earliest biblical events. A case in point is the debate over the date of the Exodus. While some scholars believe that the Exodus occurred during the thirteenth century B.C., others accept an earlier date during the fifteenth century B.C.[10] How you look at the evidence will depend on the date chosen for the Exodus.

According to archaeologists, the city of Jericho was uninhabited during the thirteenth century B.C. For those accepting the later date for the Exodus, this is a significant problem since it was empty at the time Joshua was supposed to have been capturing the city.[11] On the other hand, those who accept the earlier date for the Exodus believe that Joshua attacked Jericho about 1400 B.C. At this time, some archaeologists have said that the city was destroyed during a siege.[12]

The problem with trying to prove the Bible with archaeology is that neither gives a complete picture. The Bible gives us a view of history as it relates to God's plan for salvation. What are tremendously essential events in the Bible, such as the birth of Jesus Christ, would appear to the world as unimportant and irrelevant, just another poor child born into the world. Likewise, what may

---

10 As will probably be clear from the discussion that follows, this author accepts the earlier date for the Exodus. A presentation of the case for the earlier date can be found in: Gleason L. Archer, *A Survey of Old Testament Introduction* (Chicago: Moody Press, 1974) pp. 230-241, also pp. 221-225. For a discussion supporting the later date see: J. A. Thompson, *The Bible and Archaeology 3rd edition* (Grand Rapids: Eerdmans, 1982) pp. 60-64.

11 Magnus Magnusson, *Archaeology of the Bible* (New York: Simon and Schuster, 1977) p. 94.

12 Gleason L. Archer, *Encyclopedia of Bible Difficulties* (Grand Rapids: Zondervan, 1982) p. 195.
     also
     Bryant Wood, *Did the Israelites Conquer Jericho? A New Look at the Archaeological Evidence Biblical Archaeology Review*, Mar./Apr. 1990.

be a significant event for archaeology may not even be mentioned in the Bible.

Archaeology is like a large puzzle where we have only a few pieces. As we put the pieces together, patterns begin to form. As more pieces are found, the picture usually becomes more apparent. Still, sometimes a new piece only seems to confuse the picture, showing that something is out of place and that we need to reevaluate our theories.

When we put the views of history provided by archaeology and the Bible together, asking one to prove the other, it is not surprising that we find there is no complete match, that gaps exist, and that, in fact, there are even some differences.

Sometimes the problem is in our understanding of a biblical passage or our translation of an ancient term. In both of these areas, archaeology has dramatically increased our understanding of the Bible. Sometimes the problem is in the findings of archaeology. Yet as we find more "pieces" and get more of the picture, archaeology is moving closer to confirming the Bible's accounts.

ARCHAEOLOGY AND THE PATRIARCHS

To illustrate how archaeological discoveries have supported the Bible, let us look at the lives of the patriarchs as recorded in the book of Genesis. I chose the patriarchs because they are the oldest accounts in the Bible that somewhat fit into the historical framework, that is, events that we can assign some sort of date.

While we can begin to assign dates, scholars still disagree. Still, we can compare archaeological data from the proposed periods. Because of the early date at which these events were supposed to have taken place, many have considered them to be the fabrication of later writers attempting to explain the origins of the Hebrew religion.

The account of the patriarchs begins in the twelfth chapter of Genesis. God tells Abram, whose name was later changed to the more familiar Abraham, "Leave your country, your people and your father's household and go to the land I will show you " (Genesis 12:1). Even though we can place this account into a historical framework, the exact time during which Abraham lived is still in question.

If they don't believe him to be a complete fabrication, most liberal scholars believe that he lived in the latter part of the fifteenth century B.C.[13] On the other hand, most conservative scholars would place Abraham much earlier, during the end of the third millennium or the beginning of the second. This difference, as we shall see, becomes significant when considering the accuracy of the accounts recorded in Genesis.

When nineteenth-century scholars tried to compare archaeology and the Bible, they were confronted with the fact that there was very little in the discoveries of archaeologists that related to, much less confirmed, the Bible. Archaeology, however, was still a new science. Rather than waiting for further evidence, many began to denounce the Bible as being in error and unreliable.

Now that the findings of archaeology have significantly increased, when we compare the narrative of the patriarchs to these findings, we find the patriarchs fit very well into the early part of the Middle Bronze Age (1950-1750 B.C.).

Among the things archaeologists have confirmed, the cities mentioned in Genesis during the time of the patriarchs, such as Bethel, Shechem, and Hebron, were inhabited during this period. Names found in Genesis, such as Abram, Terah, Nahor, and Laban, have also been found in the writings from this period. While the patriarchal accounts were once accused of incorrectly mentioning camels, we now know camels were domesticated and used during this period.[14]

More importantly, the social order and customs described in the patriarchal accounts are very similar to those found during the

13   John H Hayes, *Introduction to the Bible* (Philadelphia: Westminster Press, 1971) p. 56.

14   J. A. Thompson, *The Bible and Archaeology 3rd edition* (Grand Rapids: Eerdmans, 1982) pp. 28-9.

Middle Bronze Age. In Genesis 16, we have the account of Sarai, unable to have any children herself, telling her husband to sleep with her maidservant so that he might have a child.

To us, this seems bizarre and peculiar thing to do. Many have wondered why Sarai did this. Now we know what Sarai did was standard at the time. Archaeologists have even found it in marriage contracts of the period. If the wife did not have a child, it was her responsibility to provide her husband with a maidservant so he could have a son.[15]

Sarai was not acting strangely; she was only carrying out the customs of her day. How would a later writer have known about such a custom? And even if he knew, would a later writer have presented such a strange practice so casually with no explanation or commentary? The writer of this account lived when readers took this custom for granted; it was the proper thing for a wife to do.

Many parallels exist between the customs of the Middle Bronze Age and the patriarchal accounts in Genesis. Some of these, at first, seem to be very trivial. Yet, as such, they make an even stronger case for the accuracy of the overall account. The more trivial the point, the more likely a later writer would overlook it. Lot's door is an example.

In Genesis 19, we have the account of Lot shutting the door to his house and a crowd moving trying to break it down. What is so important about a door? Excavations of Middle Bronze Age cities have shown that large, heavy doors were widespread, most likely because of the lack of protection from any governmental structure.

When liberal scholars date these stories, local governments provided enough protection that houses did not need doors. Cities excavated from this later period show that, rather than a door, the entrance to a house was a simple archway, possibly covered with a curtain. This inconsistency in the liberal position has prompted Joseph Free to ask:

---

15 D. J. Wiseman, *Archaeology and the Old Testament* in *The Expositor's Bible Commentary* ed. Frank E Gaebelein (Grand Rapids, MI: Zondervan, 1979) p. 316.

Lot's heavy door fits precisely in this period. The
critics, however, date the writing of the account of Abraham in the ninth and eighth centuries B.C. How did the
writer know the conditions a thousand years or more
before his time?[16]

We could ask: If the writer got such a seemingly insignificant
detail correct, is it not more likely that he also got the significant
ones correct?

One of the more criticized events in the account of the patriarchs is Abraham's rescue of Lot in Genesis 14. This account
describes a war among opposing coalitions of kings. The terms
'war' and 'kings' are probably misleading, given the sizes of 'kingdoms' and 'armies,' for they were pretty small by modern standards.
Today, they would be leaders and battles.

Early liberal scholars believed these kings to be total fabrications. From documents discovered while excavating the ancient
Syrian city of Mari, destroyed during the eighteenth century B.C.,
we now know that coalitions among kings, such as described in
Genesis 14, did exist during this period. The names of the kings
are now also known to have been familiar names of kings for the
Middle Bronze Age, with some of them, like Arioch, occurring
only during this period.

While archeologists have not found direct confirmation of this
war, this is hardly surprising. Again, "wars" during this period were
relatively small by today's standards. What we can say is, based on
what we now know, this war does fit well within the period of the
Middle Bronze Age.[17]

The discoveries of archaeology also support the account of
Joseph in Egypt.[18] We have, for instance, found that inflation is

16 Joseph P Free, *Archaeology and Bible History* (Wheaton Ill: Van Kamper
    Press, 1950) p. 63.

17 Gleason L Archer Jr., *A Survey of Old Testament Introduction* (Chicago:
    Moody Press, 1994) pp. 220-221.

18 As with the Exodus, there is a debate over the date of Joseph. Basically
    this centers around whether Joseph was in Egypt during the rule of the
    Hyskos, or whether he was there earlier. Again, this author accepts the
    earlier date. A presentation of the case for the earlier date can be found

not confined to modern times and that the price of slaves, as with everything else, experienced cost increases. Genesis says Joseph's brothers sold him into slavery for 20 silver shekels. This was the right price for slaves during the eighteenth century B.C.[19] Before this, the price was lower, while after, it was higher.

The Wilbur Papyri is a listing of about 100 slaves dating from 1740 B.C. It shows slaves could rise to positions of power and influence. About half the slaves on the list were Semites, and some had risen to higher positions. Donald Wiseman summed up the support for the Joseph account as,

> The use of contemporarily attested technical terms (e.g., 'butler,' 'baker' as courtiers [saris]), the prison procedure, and proper names, parallels with the Egyptian Tale of Two Brothers, the court etiquette (41:14), the investiture, and economic milieu all bear witness to the validity of the Joseph narratives.[20]

While we have not found direct confirmation of the patriarchal accounts, we can not reasonably expect such confirmation. When we examine the accounts of the patriarchs in light of recent archaeological discoveries, we find that they accurately describe the times and customs of the period.

POTENTIAL PROBLEMS

As we mentioned earlier, there are a few places where the accounts in the Bible still conflict with archeological data. Two of the most well-known and cited instances are the number of people in the Exodus and Joshua's destruction of the city of Ai.

in: Gleason L. Archer, *A Survey of Old Testament Introduction* (Chicago: Moody Press, 1974) pp. 221-225. For a discussion supporting the later date see: J. A. Thompson, *The Bible and Archaeology 3rd edition* (Grand Rapids: Eerdmans, 1982) pp. 41-55.

19 D. J. Wiseman, *Archaeology and the Old Testament* in *The Expositor's Bible Commentary* ed. Frank E Gaebelein (Grand Rapids, MI: Zondervan, 1979) p. 317.

20 D. J. Wiseman, *Archaeology and the Old Testament* in *The Expositor's Bible Commentary* ed. Frank E Gaebelein (Grand Rapids, MI: Zondervan, 1979) p. 317 .

Moses records that the number of men of fighting age who left Egypt during the Exodus was 603,550.[21] When we allow for the women and children, this brings the total number of people who left Egypt during the Exodus to over two million.

Archaeologists point out that the Sinai couldn't have supported that many people. Magnus Magnusson, in his book *Archaeology of the Bible*, wrote concerning this large number of men,

> this implies that the host of refugees must have numbered at least two million – a figure that stretches even the most sympathetic credulity. It is simply not believable that a host of this size could have survived in the wilderness for forty years, as the Bible claims.[22][19]

Bernhard Anderson, Professor of Old Testament Theology at Princeton Theological Seminary, concludes that,

> Clearly, the Delta area could not have accommodated so many Hebrews and their animals, and the wilderness of southern Canaan could not have supported them. Undoubtedly the band of slaves was comparatively small.[23]

There was not enough food or water in the desert, so these scholars concluded that this number could not possibly be correct.

Conservative scholars have suggested several solutions to this problem. Some think that the translation of Hebrew at this point is incorrect. While there are many theories about the correct translation, most center around the Hebrew word *'elep*, normally translated as "thousand." Some have pointed to passages such as Joshua 22:14, where the same word means "a family division," as evidence that the word can have other meanings.[24]

---

21 See Exodus 15:22-24, 16:2-3, 17:1-3 Numbers 11:4-6, 20:2-5.

22 Magnus Magnusson, *Archaeology of the Bible* (New York: Simon and Schuster, 1977) p. 94.

23 Bernhard W. Anderson, *Understanding the Old Testament* (Englewood Cliffs, New Jersey: Prentice-Hall, 1975) p. 67.

24 It is not uncommon for words to have different meanings depending on the context. For instance, the English word can might mean: ability ("I can run"); a container ("I put it in the can"); or to be fired ("I was canned").

Another theory suggested by Rev. John Wenham points out that Hebrew words were initially written without vowels. Without vowels, '*elep* would have been written as '*lp*. This word could easily have been confused with another Hebrew word, '*allup*,' translated as chief, commander, or armed man.

Wenham's theory is that the number of men of fighting age recorded for the tribe of Simeon, for example, may originally have been written as "57 '*lp*; 2 '*lp* 3 hundred" to indicate 57 armed men (officers) and 2300 soldiers. As Wenham points out,

> Not realizing that '*lp* in one case meant "armed man" and in the other "thousand," this was tidied up to read 59,300. When these figures are carefully decoded, a remarkably clear picture of the whole military organization emerges. The total fighting force is some 18,000 which would probably mean a figure of about 72,000 for the whole migration.[25]

The figure of 72,000 for the Exodus is significantly lower than the two million in traditional translations and would not encounter the same objections.

Other theories come up with similar but slightly different numbers. Then there is the issue of how the ancient writers understood these numbers. Did these writers understand these numbers the same way we do? In short, do these large numbers result from an error made by the writers or a misunderstanding on our part?

Other conservative scholars acknowledge the problem of the large numbers. They agree that the number of people is too large to have lived off the Sinai. But they point out that the Bible also acknowledges this fact.

Throughout their wandering in the wilderness, the Israelites found that the food and water available in the desert would not support them.[26] God supported the Israelites at these times by pro-

---

25 John Wenham, *The Large Numbers of the Old Testament* in *Eerdmans' Handbook to the Bible* ed. David Alexander and Pat Alexander (Grand Rapids, MI: Eerdmans, 1973) p. 192.

26 See Exodus 15:22-24, 16:2-3, 17:1-3 Numbers 11:4-6, 20:2-5.

viding them with food (manna) and water. Gleason Archer has written that,

> The objection that the natural resources of the Sinai desert could never have supported two million people or more for a period of forty years' wandering is absolutely valid. But it completely overlooks what the Pentateuch makes abundantly clear: Israel did not receive its food and drink from the ordinary natural resources of the Sinai terrain... The God who led the Israelites in the pillar of cloud was the one who supplied them with their nourishment by way of supernatural intervention.[27]

By natural means, two million people could not have lived for forty years in the Sinai, but by the power of God, it was possible. If one rejects the supernatural and believes that it is impossible that God sent manna to eat or to provide water to drink, as many critics do, these large numbers present a real problem. So the problem is not between archaeology and the Bible; it is the supernatural's existence and God's ability to perform miracles. We will examine these issues in more detail in the next book in this series.[28]

Another major conflict between archaeology and the Bible is in the account in Joshua chapters seven and eight concerning the destruction of the city of Ai. Archaeological findings show that Ai was uninhabited during both times proposed for the conquest (1406 B.C. and 1250 B.C.). As Magnusson writes concerning the excavations of the city of Ai:

> The outcome of these excavations is simply stated: there was a major fortified city at Ai at the start of the Early Bronze Age (c. 3000 B.C.) which, after several destructions and rebuilding, was violently destroyed by some unknown aggressor around 2400 B.C. and abandoned. Thereafter there was no further occupation of the site until the start of the Iron Age, around 1200 B.C.,

---

27 Gleason Archer, *Encyclopedia of Bible Difficulties* (Grand Rapids: Zondervan, 1982) p. 130.

28 Elgin Hushbeck, *Christianity and Secularism, Consider Christinity Series Volume 2* (Gonzalez, Forida: Energion).

when it gradually began to be settled by squatters and
tent-dwellers who built an unwalled village there.[29]

According to the biblical account, Joshua lost the first battle
at Ai. Only on the second attempt did he capture and burn the
city. Unless an uninhabited city defeated Joshua's army, something
would seem wrong.

Ai, which in Hebrew means the ruin, is usually identified with
et-Tell, a ruin about ten miles north of Jerusalem and two miles to
the east of the city of Bethel. This identification, however, is not
universally accepted.

Some have pointed out that the description of Ai in the Bible
does not correspond with et-Tell. Joshua 7:3 implies that Ai was
a small community since Israelites felt they only needed to send a
fraction of their fighting force. The city at et-Tell was large.

In Joshua, we read that the ruins of Ai were visible "to this
day" (Joshua 8:28). In contrast, the ruins at et-Tell were not visible
during the period after the conquest. According to Joshua 8:11, a
broad valley was north of Ai, yet no such valley exists to the north
of et-Tell. Finally, Joshua 7:5 speaks of a slope (Hebrew: morad)
between Ai and Jericho. Again, no such feature exists between et-
Tell and Jericho.[30]

So there are good reasons to believe that et-Tell is not the city
of Ai mentioned in the book of Joshua. While there would appear
to be a discrepancy between et-Tell and the biblical description of
Ai's destruction, it is not sure that these two places are the same.

When one considers all the other instances where critics
claimed that archaeology had disproven the Bible, only to be wrong
as more information was discovered, is it not reasonable to wait for
further information before rejecting the biblical account?

Since the writing of the preceding paragraphs, it would seem
the critics were wrong yet again. The search for Ai continued, and

---

29 Magnus Magnusson, *Archaeology of the Bible* (New York: Simon and
Schuster, 1977) p. 89.

30 Gleason L. Archer, *A Survey of Old Testament Introduction* (Chicago:
Moody Press, 1974) pp. 238-9.

excavations at another site matching the biblical description yielded positive results. These excavations show that Khirbert el-Maqatir was the site of a small fortress in the 15th century B.C., the earlier of the two dates proposed for the Exodus. This fortress was attacked, destroyed by fire, and not rebuilt.

> The geography and archaeology of Khirbet el-Maqatir accord with the descriptions of Ai in Joshua 7–8. The identification of Khirbet el-Maqatir as the Ai of Joshua's time resolves the problems of chronology and location that ensued from Callaway's excavation at et-Tell.[31]

In real life, things are usually much more complicated than we might initially believe. Life does not always fit into nice neat categories that can be quickly summarized. At one time, critics claimed Daniel was wrong when he said that Belshazzar was the last ruler of Babylon (Daniel 5:30). Other ancient writers said that Nabonidus was the last ruler of Babylon.

It seemed that someone was wrong, and the critics naturally assumed it must have been Daniel. As it turns out, both accounts are correct. The situation in the Babylonian empire's closing days was much more complicated than just a king ruling his empire.

Shortly after Nabonidus became king, he captured the oasis city of Teima in what is now the Northwest part of Saudi Arabia. Nabonidus liked the place so much that he decided to settle down there. His decision caused problems since Nabonidus still wanted to remain king. He needed someone to take care of the actual running of the empire, whose capital was still in Babylon, so Nabonidus appointed his son, Belshazzar.[32]

In a very real sense, both Nabonidus and Belshazzar were the last rulers of Babylon. For the historian, Nabonidus was the official king when Babylon fell and is recorded as such by the ancient writers. Yet for someone actually living in Babylon when it fell,

---

31   Scott Stripling & Mark Hassler, *A Clear Conquest Pattern Evidence,* Feb, 16, 2019, https://patternsofevidence.com/2019/02/16/clear-conquest-pattern/.

32   J. A. Thompson, *The Bible and Archaeology 3rd edition* (Grand Rapids: Eerdmans, 1982) pp. 197-9.

as Daniel was, the ruler he would have written about would have been Belshazzar.[33] We can see that Daniel understood the situation when he wrote about Belshazzar's promise to make him "the third highest ruler in the kingdom" (Daniel 5:16). He would be third after Nabonidus and Belshazzar.

Once again, we ask: How would a later author have known the details of the Babylonian court unless he was present? A later author would have read the same ancient writers as the early critics if he had done some research. Thus a later writer would have said Nabonidus, not Belshazzar, was the ruler of Babylon.

While archaeology does not provide proof for the Hebrew Scripture, we have seen that it has provided a great deal of support for its accuracy. In the few places where archaeology and the Bible conflict, it is not clear where the problem is. Nowhere has archaeology shown the Bible to be definitely in error. Does archaeology support the historical accuracy of the Hebrew Scripture? Yes.

ARCHAEOLOGY AND THE NEW TESTAMENT

When we come to the New Testament, we see a similar situation to the Hebrew Scriptures. Nineteenth-century critics of the Bible essentially wrote off the New Testament as religiously motivated fabrications. They believed it contained very little, if anything, of historical value.

A large part of modern liberal scholarship dealing with the New Testament is trying to extract the "historical Jesus" out of the text. As with the Hebrew Scripture, discoveries by archaeologists have caused problems for those who have maintained such skeptical views. As the noted archaeologist, W. F. Albright put it in 1964,

> In other words, all radical schools in New Testament criticism which have existed in the past or which exist today are prearchaeological, and are, therefore,

---

33 Gleason L. Archer, *Daniel* in *The Expositor's Bible Commentary* ed. Frank E Gaebelein (Grand Rapids, MI: Zondervan, 1979) Vol. 7 pp. 4-6.

> since they were built *in der Luft* ("in the air"), quite anti-
> quated today.[34]

An excellent example of this change involves the noted archaeologist Sir William Ramsay. At the schools Sir Ramsay attended,
liberal theology, with its general disregard for the historical accuracy
of the biblical accounts, was taught as the only acceptable "scientific" view of the Bible. This teaching convinced Sir Ramsay that,
as historical documents, he could not trust the books of the New
Testament.

Sir Ramsay undertook a topographical study of Asia Minor
during the first century A.D. Yet he quickly discovered a severe
lack of source material from that period, and he had little choice
but to use the book of Acts.

Even though he believed that Acts, like the rest of the Bible,
could not be relied upon in historical matters, it was at least better
than nothing. To his surprise, Sir Ramsay found the book of Acts
to be amazingly accurate. He recorded his change of attitude as
follows,

> I may fairly claim to have entered on this investi-
> gation without any prejudice in favor of the conclusion
> which I shall now attempt to justify to the reader. On the
> contrary, I began with a mind unfavorable to it, for the
> ingenuity and apparent completeness of the Tubingen
> theory had at one time quite convinced me. It did not
> lie then in my line of life to investigate the subject mi-
> nutely; but more recently I found myself often brought
> in contact with the Book of *Acts* as an authority for the
> topography, antiquities, and society of Asia Minor. It
> was gradually borne in upon me that in various details
> the narrative showed marvelous truth. In fact, begin-
> ning with the fixed idea that the work was essentially a
> second century composition, and never relying on its
> evidence as trustworthy for first century conditions, I
> gradually came to find it a useful ally in some obscure
> and difficult investigations.[35]

---

34 W. F. Albright, *The Teacher's Yoke* p. 29 as quoted in Edwin M. Yamauchi,
Archaeology and the New Testament in *The Expositor's Bible Commentary* ed.
Frank E Gaebelein (Grand Rapids, MI: Zondervan, 1979) Vol. 1 p. 647.

35 Sir William Ramsay, *St. Paul the Traveler and the Roman Citizen* (New
York: G.P. Putman's Sons, 1896) pp. 7-8.

After many years of study, Sir Ramsay summed up his opinion of Luke, the author of Acts, as,

> a historian of the first rank; not merely are his statements of fact trustworthy, he was possessed of the true historical sense; he fixes his mind on the idea and plan that rules in the evolution of history; and proportions the scale of his treatment to the importance of each incident... In short, this author should be placed along with the very greatest of historians.[36]

Many of Luke's statements, once believed to have been wrong, are now correct with recent discoveries. For example, critics believed Luke made a mistake when he said that the city of Iconium was not part of Lycaonia.[37] This conclusion was based, in large part, on the testimony of ancient writers mentioning Iconium, along with Lystra, as part of Lycaonia during this period. As with Daniel, it seemed that someone was wrong, and the critics naturally concluded that it must have been Luke.

As it turned out, things were again not as straightforward as the early critics assumed. Iconium was on the border of Phrygia and very close to the city of Lystra. As political boundaries often are, this border was somewhat artificial, and Iconium and Lystra had very close ties.

With these ties, it is easy to see why ancient writers connected the two. Still, politically we now know that Luke was correct, for Iconium was part of the administrative district of Phrygia during this period.[38] It was the discovery of this fact that first led Sir Ramsay to begin reconsidering the historical reliability of Luke.[39]

Luke's attention to detail is such that it is hard to see how he could have done this without careful research or being an eyewitness to the events he describes. Note his descriptions of the leader

---

36 Sir William Ramsay, *The Bearing of Recent Discovery on the Trustworthiness of the New Testament* (London: Hodden and Stoughton, 1915) p. 222.

37 Luke 14:1,6.

38 R. K. Harrison, *Archaeology of the New Testament* (New York: Association Press, 1964) p. 37.

39 J. A. Thompson, *The Bible and Archaeology 3rd edition* (Grand Rapids: Eerdmans, 1982) pp. 393.

of the island of Malta in Acts 28. Luke describes Publius as the "first man" (*protos, πρώτῳ)* of the island (Acts 28:7). The term that Luke uses is not common, but Luke accurately uses it in this case.

Throughout his writings, Luke is very precise in his choice of titles for the leaders he mentions. This precision was not as easy a task as it may seem at first glance. During the first century, these titles changed from place to place and even varied from ruler to ruler.

The island of Cyprus, which Paul visited on his first missionary journey, had four types of Roman governments within the space of 35 years.[40] It would have been easy to make a mistake unless he was meticulous. As R. K. Harrison, Professor of Old Testament at Wycliffe College has pointed out,

> Some of the most impressive examples of Lukan accuracy consist of the titles of Imperial officials recorded in his writings. That these reflect the contemporary scene is evident from the fact that the titles of provincial governors changed without warning when the status of particular provinces was altered.[41]

Why would Luke make an effort to be so precise if historical accuracy was of no concern? Perhaps the most questioned event recorded by Luke is the occurrence of a census at the time of the birth of Jesus. According to Luke:

> In those days Caesar Augustus issued a decree that a census should be taken of the entire Roman world. (This was the first census that took place while Quirinius was governor of Syria.) And everyone went to his own town to register. (Luke 2:1-3)

Since we know that Joseph and Mary took Jesus to Egypt to await the death of King Herod, who died in 4 B.C., we know that Jesus must have been born before this date. The Jewish historian Josephus mentions that Quirinius was appointed to take a census. The problem arises because the census mentioned by Josephus

---

40   J. A. Thompson, *The Bible and Archaeology 3rd edition* (Grand Rapids: Eerdmans, 1982) pp.391.

41   R. K. Harrison, Archaeology of the New Testament (New York: Association Press, 1964) p. 34.

occurred in A.D. 6 or 7. Yet, Luke states that a census occurred around 7 or 6 B.C.

The solution for this difference in dates can be seen in Luke's statement that this was the first census for Quirinius. If Luke takes the time to point out that this census was the first one, does it not imply that there must have been a second one? Since the Romans regularly conducted a census every fourteen years,[42] Rome likely had a census conducted at the time Luke claims.

As for Quirinius being the governor during this time, there are two possibilities. One is that Quirinius was governor twice, once around 7 B.C. and then later around A.D. 7. This view has recently found some support with the discovery of an inscription that seems to mention Quirinius as governor at an earlier date.[43]

Still, some scholars dispute this inscription's meaning, which is not accepted by all. Also, other records indicate that Saturninus was governor from 9 B.C. to 6 B.C. Quintilius Varus replaced him from 7 B.C. to A.D. 4. This left no room for a governorship for Quirinius until after A.D. 4.

A second possibility emerges when we examine the Greek text. As we have seen, Luke was very particular about using the proper titles when he referred to government leaders. The proper Greek term for the governor of a region such as Syria at this time would have been *legatus* (λεγάτος). But Luke does not use this term. Instead, he uses the term *hegemoneuontos* (ἡγεμονεύοντος), which means to lead or to be in charge. As Gleason Archer has stated, Quirinius,

> was therefore a highly placed military figure in the Near East in the closing years of the reign of Herod the Great. In order to secure efficiency and dispatch, it may well have been that Augustus put Quirinius in charge of the census-enrollment in the region of Syria just at the transition period between the close of Saturninus's

---

42 J. A. Thompson, The Bible and Archaeology 3rd edition (Grand Rapids: Eerdmans, 1982) pp.387.

43 J. A. Thompson, The Bible and Archaeology 3rd edition (Grand Rapids: Eerdmans, 1982) pp.388.

administration and the beginning of Varus's term of
service in 7 B.C.[44]

Critics have also pointed to Luke's claim that people had to
return to their towns. Many believed this was simply a literary
device used by Luke so that Jesus could be born in Bethlehem. Yet
we find this practice also has been confirmed by archaeology. A
papyrus found in Egypt gives the instructions for a census. Among
the instructions was a requirement for people to "return home in
order to comply with the customary ordinance of enrollment."[45]

We find that the account of the census in Luke has not been
disproven but rather fits well with what we know about that period.
The Romans regularly conducted a census, and Luke's census was
the right time for one to have occurred. Quirinius could very well
have been in charge of Syria's census in 6 B.C. The Romans sometimes required that people return to their homes for the census.
Therefore, there is little reason to doubt Luke's account.

Most of the New Testament deals with events that do not easily lend themselves to archeological confirmation. Luke, writing
in the book of Acts, states that when Paul preached in the city of
Lystra, he was taken out of the city, stoned, and left for dead (Acts
14:8-20). Other than the city of Lystra existed during this time,
supporting evidence for such an event would be hard to come by.

Nevertheless, a limited amount of support exists for several
statements in the New Testament. We know that Pontius Pilate
was governor of Judea from A.D. 26 to A.D. 36. We see some of
the people mentioned in the New Testament in documents and
inscriptions of the period.

At the end of his letter to the Romans, Paul mentions one
"Erastus, who is the city's director of public works" (Romans
16:23). Paul wrote this letter from the city of Corinth. In this
city, archaeologists have found a stone with an inscription that says,

---

44   Gleason L. Archer, Encyclopedia of Bible Difficulties (Grand Rapids:
     Zondervan, 1982) p. 366.
45   F. F. Bruce, *The New Testament Documents: Are They Reliable?* (Dower
     Grove Ill: Inter-Varsity Press, 1943) p. 86.

> Erastus, in commemoration of his aedileship (cu-
> ratorship of public buildings), laid this pavement at his
> own expense.[46]

Perhaps one of the most remarkable finds of this sort occurred in 1992, with the accidental discovery of the family tomb
of Caiaphas still containing his body. While the historical existence of Caiaphas was not questioned, this discovery marks the first
instance of a person mentioned in New Testament being found.
It also emphasizes that important discoveries still remain buried,
waiting to be found.

Like the Hebrew Scriptures, we can compare the New Testament accounts with the period's customs. Unlike the Hebrew
Scriptures, which covers 1000 years, the New Testament covers
only about 70 years (approximately A.D. 26 - A.D. 95). Rather
than changes in customs over time, we must look at differences
due to location. This examination is what Sir Ramsay did, and it
convinced him of the accuracy of Luke.

Luke records that while Paul was on his second missionary
journey, he came to Athens. While there, Paul carried on his discussions "in the marketplace day by day with those who happened
to be there" (Acts 17:17). However, when he was in the city of
Ephesus while on his third missionary journey, he "had discussions
daily in the lecture hall of Tyrannus" (Acts 19:9). In Athens, Luke
says Paul carried on his discussions in the marketplace. In Ephesus,
these took place in a lecture hall. This is precisely in accordance
with the local customs of each location[47] and shows that Luke was
concerned with accurately recording even such seemingly insignificant details.

---

46   F. F. Bruce, *Jesus and Paul, Places They Knew* (Nashville: Thomas Nelson,
     1981) p. 104.

47   J. A. Thompson, *The Bible and Archaeology 3rd edition* (Grand Rapids:
     Eerdmans, 1982) pp. 397.

CONCLUSION

We have seen that, where possible, archaeology has provided an amazing amount of support for the Bible. Most of the support has been in the area of background details. Still, we should remember that the critics claim these stories are religious myths and that the writers had no interest in actual history. If the writers of the Bible were only recording myths, why did they care to get even the little details correct?

If they were writing long after the events they describe, how did the writers know the customs and conditions of the earlier time? That the background details are correct is a strong argument for the veracity of the overall account. While we cannot say that archaeology has proven the biblical accounts, we can say that archaeology has gone a long way toward refuting the claim that it is religious fiction. In many ways, it demonstrates the historical reliability of both the Old and New Testaments.

4

SCIENCE VS RELIGION?

*Extinguished theologians lie about the cradle of every
science as the strangled snakes beside that of Hercules.
(Thomas Huxley)*

JOHANNES KEPLER HAD PLANNED on becoming a minister. But like so many others, Kepler's plans were superseded by circumstances. In 1594, Kepler left the University at Tubingen to teach mathematics at a Lutheran high school in Graz, Austria. Kepler was not a very good teacher, and his thoughts tended to wander. Such was the case one summer day in 1595. During one of his lectures, an idea suddenly struck him. While wrong, the idea was to change Kepler's life and our understanding of the universe.

In school, Kepler had been fortunate to have a teacher who accepted and taught the recent theory of Copernicus that the six planets revolved in circles around the Sun. As a mathematics teacher, Kepler was also well aware that the ancient Greeks had shown that there were only five regular or Platonic solids[1] and that these solids fit into a sphere in a unique way. Kepler's idea was simple: There are only six planets and five regular solids. What if the two are related?

Of course, now we know that there are actually nine planets or, by the latest thinking, 8 with 5 Dwarf Planets, so the basis for Kepler's theory was wrong. But William Herschel would not discover the seventh planet, Uranus, for another 186 years. Herschel had a telescope, something else still in the future for Kepler.

---

1   Platonic solids are those in which all the sides are identical. For example:
a cube is made up of six identical squares and is therefore a regular or
Platonic solid.

So at the time, Kepler's theory seemed as good as any other, and he set out to prove it. His first step was to get financial backing to build an elaborate solar system model made of silver and jewels. When this fell through, he settled for models made of paper.

Hour after hour, day after day, Kepler tried to work out the mathematics of his new theory, which he called the *Cosmographic Mystery*. He wanted to match his theory's predictions to the planets' actual movement as astronomers had recorded them. In this, Kepler hoped to "transfer the whole of astronomy from fictitious circles to natural causes"[2] and reveal the hand of God in the creation. The problem was the models he made never quite matched the recorded positions of the planets.

Kepler felt that perhaps the records of the astronomers were in error. At that time, Tycho Brahe, the Danish astronomer who had developed special instruments for the task, kept the best records of the movement of the planets. Brahe's records were thirty times more accurate than earlier astronomers. So in 1600, Kepler went to work for Brahe. The following year Brahe died, leaving all his records to Kepler.

Now Kepler had what he needed: records accurate enough to prove his theories were correct. Over the next four years, Kepler calculated orbit after orbit to fit Brahe's observations of the planet Mars into his theories. Today, no one would even consider such a task without a computer. Kepler did not even have a table of logarithms.

Kepler was able to get closer to a mathematical description of the orbit of Mars than anyone before him. He could match ten of Brahe's observations to within two minutes of arc or about 1/10,000 of the diameter of a circle. Two other measurements Kepler matched to within eight minutes of arc. Kepler could ignore a two-minute error as too small for Brahe to have measured accurately. The eight minutes of arc was another story. Before

---

2   Quoted in: Roy Peacock, *A Brief History of Eternity* (Wheaton, IL: Crossway Books, 1990) p. 35.

Brahe, Kepler could ignore eight minutes of arc as an error in measurement, but not after.

Abandoning his theories, Kepler took a completely different approach. Instead of a circle, what if the orbits were an ellipse? Things finally began to fall into place. After many years of research and endless calculations, Kepler discovered the three laws of planetary motion that now bear his name.

For Kepler, this was also a spiritual discovery. Through his discovery, Kepler gained a better understanding of the workings of the universe, and in so doing, he felt that he had caught a glimpse of the Creator. He wrote, "O God, I am thinking thy thoughts after thee."[3]

Kepler's belief that his scientific discovery brought him closer to God was not really that unusual. Before the nineteenth century, many saw science and Christianity as two separate paths to the same goal: knowledge of God.

In fact, the roots of modern science lie within the Christian religion. During the Renaissance and Reformation, Christians stressed God's role as a rational Creator. They believed as a rational Creator, his creation would also be rational and well-ordered. Just as you can learn about a painter by studying their paintings, they believed that by studying creation, you could better understand the Creator.

The belief that an intelligent, rational Creator created the universe encouraged the development of science in another way: it made it intellectually possible. Suppose you believe that the universe is an irrational place where things happen for no apparent reason. In that case, you will not likely spend much time figuring out how it all works.

In many Eastern cultures, there was a belief that the universe is, to some extent, an illusion and not very important. This view of the universe played a significant role in science's development, or non-development, in places like China. Even though many

3   Quoted in: Roy Peacock, *A Brief History of Eternity* (Wheaton, IL: Crossway Books, 1990) p. 38.

important discoveries and inventions, like gunpowder and print-
ing, were first made in China, they had a much smaller impact on
Eastern cultures than when introduced into the West.

The philosopher Francis Schaeffer summed up this lack of
tension between religion and science at the beginning of the Scientific Revolution,

> The rise of modern science did not conflict with
> what the Bible teaches; indeed, at a crucial point the Sci-
> entific Revolution rested upon what the Bible teaches.
> Both Alfred North Whitehead (1861-1947) and J. Robert
> Oppenheimer (1904-1967) have stressed that modern
> science was born out of the Christian world view.[4]

When we look at the relationship between Christianity and
science at the beginning of the Scientific Revolution, we find a
unity unknown in modern times. Christianity and science were
so closely intertwined that many scientific beliefs began to take
on the status of religious doctrines. This close relationship led to
problems. The conflict between the Catholic Church and Galileo
is a classic example.

GALILEO

Thomas Aquinas was a large quiet man. To those who did not
know him well, he seemed so slow, both physically and intellectually, that he earned the title of "*The Dumb Ox.*" Yet during the
thirteenth century, Thomas Aquinas set the intellectual direction
of the church. The influence of Aquinas was so strong that it can
still be seen in many places 700 years later.

Aquinas believed that man's fall in the Garden of Eden was
only a partial fall. The intellect, Aquinas believed, had not been
corrupted by sin. According to Aquinas,

> We must assert that the intellectual principle which
> we call the human soul is incorruptible... every intellec-
> tual substance is incorruptible.[5]

---

4   Francis A Schaeffer, *How Should We Then Live?* (Westchester, IL:
    Crossway Books, 1976) p. 132.
5   Thomas Aquinas, *Summa Theologica* Q.75 Art 6.

When a belief in an incorruptible intellect is combined with the belief in a Creator who made a rational and understandable universe, the result is philosophical, and later, scientific statements concerning nature are nearly equal to those of the Prophets. By the beginning of the seventeenth century, many of the teachings of the Greek philosophers, especially those of Aristotle, had been incorporated into the church's teachings.

In 1611, shortly after Kepler's discoveries, Galileo visited Rome to demonstrate his newest invention: an improved telescope. While there, he used it to support Copernicus' theory that the planets circled the Sun, not Earth. Galileo's pushing the new theory caused a lot of problems, particularly with the Aristotelian professors at the local universities. Before long, these professors were pressuring the Catholic Church to declare this new theory heretical.

The debate over Copernicus' theory continued over the next few years. Even though Galileo had some church leaders on his side, the final decision came down to Cardinal Robert Bellarmine, the Catholic Church's chief theologian at that time.

But Cardinal Bellarmine had another problem on his hands. The Protestant Reformation was in full swing. Consequently, Cardinal Bellarmine was not as concerned with the movement of the planets as much as whether Galileo might create a scandal that Protestants could use against the Catholic Church. So on March 5, 1616, Cardinal Bellarmine issued a decree that banned the Copernican Theory.

For many, the conflict between Galileo and the Catholic Church epitomized the conflict between science and religion. As one anti-religious website put it,

> For centuries the Christian church taught us that the Earth is flat, with four corners. When a man named Galileo had the temerity to suggest that possibly, the Earth is round, the Christian church very nearly killed him for blasphemy. Today, very few Christians still believe the Earth is flat, but it took an enormously long time for the church to admit that they were wrong.[6]

---

6   Steve Corbett, *The Fall of Relgion*, 2002, http://www.noreligion.ca/readEssay.php?eid=1.

While a prevalent view, and one that extends beyond just skeptics, there are a lot of problems with it. For one, the theories of Galileo that caused the problem had nothing to do with the shape of the earth. In fact, the idea that Galileo, or even Columbus, had to overcome a Christian teaching of a flat earth is itself a myth.

The historian Jeffrey Burton Russell has pointed out that while there have always been a few who believed in a flat earth, this has been a minority point of view. It was rejected not only by educated non-Christians but also among educated Christians. As he wrote after surveying the evidence:

> In the first fifteenth centuries of the Christian era, five writers seem to have denied the globe, and a few others were ambiguous and uninterested in the question. But the nearly unanimous scholarly opinion pronounced the earth spherical, and by the fifteenth century all doubt had disappeared... So what or who led to the Flat Error?[7]

The early roots of this myth begin with the Renaissance Humanists and their creation of another commonly accepted myth: the Dark Ages. The Renaissance Humanists saw themselves restoring the ancient glories lost with Rome's fall. As they saw history, with the fall of Rome, darkness descended upon western civilization. This darkness lasted until they came along to restore the world to its past greatness.

Protestants readily embraced this view of a Dark Ages. It corresponded with the period when the Catholic Church was dominant. Modern historians have recognized this as an overly simplistic and somewhat self-serving view of history. In reality, the period was one of considerable intellectual development that set the stage for the later Middle Ages and Renaissance.

In the first half of the nineteenth century, Washington Irving wrote about Spain, including the voyages of Columbus. Irving published this book as a serious historical work he wrote in Spain after researching the subject. Nevertheless, some of the accounts

---

7   Jeffery Burton Russel, *Inventing the Flat Earth: Columbus and the Modern Historians* (Westport, Connecticut: Praeger 1991) p. 26.

in Irving's history were as much literary fiction as his more famous creation, Rip Van Winkle.

The view of a dark age of ignorance led to the uncritical acceptance of Irving's stories about Columbus arguing against those who believed the earth was flat. The book was popular and established the myth of Columbus and the flat earth in the popular mind.

This myth was then reinforced in the academic world by the writings of Antonie-Jean Letronne, who saw the Dark Ages as a time of ignorance governed by religion. He saw the end of the Dark Ages as the triumph of reason and science over religion. The flat earth myth fits perfectly with this view.

When the conflict between Science and Religion began to emerge in the latter part of the nineteenth century, claims about the Dark Ages and Flat Earth were too tempting a club to ignore. So critics embraced them uncritically and propagated them even further.

As a result, even in the twenty-first century, it is not uncommon to see modern critics of religion attacking the "myth of religion" using these myths. They claim that religion could be taking us back to the Dark Ages or equating Christians with those who believed in a flat earth.

While the conflict between Galileo and the Catholic Church was real enough, its recounting has been strongly influenced and thus exaggerated by these myths. As such, it often bears little resemblance to the actual events.

Dava Sobel has pointed this out in her biography of Galileo, *Galileo's Daughter.* Sobel tells his life story through a collection of letters written by his daughter Suor Maria Celeste. These letters,

> recolor the personality and conflict of a mythic figure, whose seventeenth-century clash with Catholic doctrines continues to define the schism between science and religion. For although science has soared beyond his quaint instruments, it is still caught in his struggle, still burdened by an impression of Galileo as a renegade who scoffed at the Bible and drew fire from a Church blind to reason... Yet the Galileo of Suor Maria Celeste's letters recognized no such division during his lifetime. He remained a good Catholic who believed in

> the power of prayer and endeavored always to conform
> his duty as a scientist with the destiny of his soul. 'What-
> ever the course of our lives,' Galileo wrote, 'we should
> receive them as the highest gift from the hand of God.'"[8]

Rather than a conflict between science and religion or even between science and Christianity, Galileo's conflict was with the Catholic Church. The Catholic Church did ban some of his works. Still, these works were published and studied by Protestants without any conflict.

In addition, Galileo had considerable support within the Catholic Church. Ultimately, this conflict was not over a difference between the Bible and a scientific discovery. Today, not even critics of the Bible try to claim that it places the Earth at the center of the universe. Rather than direct disagreement, this conflict resulted from an incorrect view of the relationship between science and the Bible.

SCIENCE VS. THE BIBLE?

From my experience, alleged conflicts between the Bible and science result from two causes. One is an incorrect understanding of the relationship between the Bible and science. The second is a lack of information, either in the biblical narrative or our scientific understanding, often both. As we shall see shortly, these often overlap.

If many conflicts result from an incorrect understanding of the relationship between science and the Bible, what is the proper one? There are four main views prevalent today concerning science and the Bible. These are:

❖ Science = knowledge   The Bible = myth
❖ Science = knowledge   The Bible = inferior knowledge
❖ Science = inferior knowledge   The Bible = knowledge
❖ Science = knowledge about   The Bible = knowledge about
                nature   God

---

8   Dava Sobel, *Galileo's Daughter,* (New York, Penguin Books, 1999) p. 11-12.

We can eliminate the first view. The Bible, when considered historically, is too accurate to be written off as myth. In addition, an extreme form of this view holding that science is the only source of truth, is self-refuting. It is self-refuting because the claim that science is the only source of truth is not, and cannot be, a scientific statement.

If it were a scientific statement, it would be circular. It would be saying that science is the only source of truth because science says it is. Therefore, the claim that science is the only source of truth must be a claim that does not come from science. As such, the claim refutes itself.

The other three views are not so quickly dealt with, and this is because we run into the problem of foundational beliefs. How you answer the question depends mainly on what pre-existing beliefs you bring to the question.

Critics of the Bible either follow a different religious belief or reject the supernatural and, thus, any belief in God. Therefore, if they don't cling to the view that the Bible is myth, they are more than likely to believe that while the Bible contains some historical knowledge, it cannot be relied upon to guide our lives. They would probably accept the second view.

Some Christians believe that while science may stumble onto some truth, the final authority in all matters is the Bible. They would accept the third position. These two positions are really very similar, separated only by their point of view. Usually, skeptics will only accept those parts of the Bible confirmed by modern science. In contrast, some Christians only accept the findings of science if the Bible has confirmed them.

The problem with both approaches is that science and Christianity deal with two completely different areas of our lives. Science concerns itself with learning about the universe's day-to-day running. How does an object fall when dropped? How does a storm produce lightning? How does a tree grow? Questions like these are the questions of science. Science deals only with the natural world and is ill-equipped to handle anything else.

A central component of science is the ability to conduct experiments. Many scientific theories fell when experiments did not yield the expected results. History, on the other hand, does not lend itself to experimentation. We cannot redo the French Revolution to test our theories.

Christianity deals with the relationship between God, as the Creator, and a single part of His creation, namely humanity. Questions addressed in the Bible include: Why are we here? Why is there suffering? Since the Bible focuses on God and His dealings with His creation, it simply does not address issues involving the day-to-day operations of the universe, except in passing.

One can easily see that the questions that concern science and the questions that concern Christianity are not the same kinds of questions. What is the scientific answer to the question: Why are we here? The reply, while possibly long and convoluted, will come down to: there is no answer; we just are.

On the other hand, the biblical answer to the question: How does an object fall when dropped ends up with a similar result – it just does. When we force science to deal with fundamentally spiritual questions or the Bible to deal with fundamentally scientific questions, problems will inevitably result.

The prophet Habakkuk described God as "His splendor was like the sunrise" (Habakkuk 3:4). Now, if we were to take this statement as a scientific description of the movement of the Sun, we would have a scientific error in the Bible. This error is because the Sun does not rise – the Earth turns. Just as clearly, Habakkuk was not attempting to make a statement concerning the motion of the Sun. Instead, he was describing the glory of God in terms understandable to his readers.

The Habakkuk quote raises an important point. The Bible is not a single book. It is a collection of books containing many different writing styles from many authors. In any evaluation of a passage, we must consider the writing style. This is especially true when we consider that many Biblical writers used a poetic style.

Poetry is an excellent way to communicate spiritual truths and descriptions of God. Suppose we try to take poetic language and extract scientific truth about nature, other than the main point intended by the author. In that case, we will undoubtedly run into trouble. As was seen in the passage from Habakkuk, trying to extract information about the motion of the Sun led quickly to error.

When attempting to relate a biblical passage to science, we must ask: What was the author trying to say? It is amazing how many supposed problems suddenly disappear when we do this.

Another problem with scientific proofs and disproofs of the Bible involves the fluid nature of science. While the Bible does not change, science, by its very nature, does. Science always leaves the door open to change and the discovery of new information. The Bible, on the other hand, was given by God. Since God already knows everything, there is no possibility of Him discovering new information. There is never a need for Him to revise the Bible.[9]

STARLIGHT, STARBRIGHT

Let us look at the Bible's description of stars as an illustration of the problems that can occur when comparing science and the Bible. People have, from the earliest times, watched the nighttime sky.[10] By the time of the Bible, the sky had been monitored and charted to an astonishing degree of accuracy. We can sometimes date historical events based on these early astronomical records.

Ancient counts of the stars ended up in the neighborhood of a few thousand. These counts agree reasonably well with the current estimates for the number of stars visible to the naked eye. Yet some have claimed that the Bible seems to tell a very different view regarding the number of stars.

---

9   This does not preclude the possibility that we may get more information that would alter our perceptions of a biblical passage. But while our understanding of a passage may need revision, the passage as originally written would not.

10   Alexander Marshack, Lunar Notation on Upper Paleolithic Remains Science Vol. 146:743-45, Nov. 6, 1964.

A very literal reading of the Bible would lead us to conclude that there are many more stars than a mere few thousand. In the book of Genesis, God told Abraham the following:

> I will surely bless you and make your descendants as numerous as the stars in the sky and as the sand on the seashore (Genesis 22:17).

In a prophecy given to the prophet Jeremiah, God said:

> I will make the descendants of David my servant and the Levities who minister before me as countless as the stars of the sky and as measureless as the sand on the seashore (Jeremiah 33:22).

In an attempt to convey God's vast knowledge, the Psalmist says that God "*determines the number of the stars and calls them each by name*" (Psalms 147:4).

In these verses and elsewhere in the Bible, the number of stars represents a vast, incomprehensible number. The stars are referred to as countless and compared to the number of grains of sand. If taken very literally, this would imply that the number of stars should be much greater than just a few thousand. Yet, astronomers during the time of Christ said that there were only about a thousand stars. This would seem to be a discrepancy if we read the Bible very literally.

We find a different story if we compare these Biblical statements about the stars to modern science. According to current estimates, there are about 100 billion stars in our galaxy alone. With an estimated 100 billion galaxies in the universe, there are about 10^{22} stars[11]. This number is close to the estimates for the total number of grains of sand in the world. Has modern science confirmed the Bible's description of the number of stars? In this example, we can see the two main problems discussed above, one with the Bible and the other with science.

---

11   The number 10^{22} is expressed in scientific notation, which is a convenient way of expressing very large numbers. Using scientific notation, 100 would be written as 10^2, 1000 would be 10^3, one billion would be 10^9. Therefore 10^{22} would be a 1 followed by 22 zeros.

For the Bible, an extremely literal reading of these verses would lead to the conclusion that there are a massive number of stars. Still, how can we be sure that the authors intended we should take their statements about stars that literally? The number of stars was not the main subject of these verses.

We should not take this argument as supporting a belief opposing a literal understanding of the Bible. We should read and understand the Bible as the authors intended it, and most of the time, that is literally. Yet clearly, not every word in the Bible is meant to be taken literally. The Bible has many literary styles, from poetry to prose.

When Peter asked Jesus if you should forgive someone as many as seven times, He responded, "I tell you, not seven times, but seventy-seven times" (Matthew 18:21,22). A very literal reading of this verse would indicate that you should forgive someone 77 times but not 78. Few would accept this understanding. As D. A. Carson wrote in his commentary on Matthew,

> Jesus is not saying that seventy-seven times is the upper limit... Rather he teaches that forgiveness of fellow members in his community of "little ones" (brothers) cannot possibly be limited by frequency or quantity.[12]

So the question is not whether we should understand the Bible literally, but when. In most cases involving theological issues, like the verse in Matthew, this is not difficult to determine from the passage's context.

The Bible is a theological book and is relatively straightforward on theological issues, at least the major ones. When trying to extract scientific information, the Bible is not as clear simply because this was not its purpose. Instead, extracting scientific information is especially difficult since such information is virtually never the main subject of the passage.

Getting scientific information out of the Bible often requires reading into a verse, something the author did not directly state.

---

12 D. A. Carson, *Matthew* in *Expositor's Bible Commentary* ed. Frank E Gaebelein.

This is always a risky proposition. In the verses mentioned above, the number of stars was not the main subject and was only used to make a point. In two verses, the point concerns the number of descendants, and in the third, the knowledge of God.

Another consideration is that since these examples needed to make a point, we can assume they had meaning to the author's intended audience. Yet, when read very literally, these verses contradicted the "science" of the period. The readers would have considered them wrong for thousands of years. It was not until A.D. 1609 that Galileo first turned a telescope to the night sky and saw many more stars.

Are we to assume that these verses should be taken literally during some periods while the author intended his readers to take them figuratively during others? If the examples used to make a point contradicted the "scientific" views of the time, the examples would not have had any meaning. Worse, they could lead to confusion.

Suppose that the prophet Habakkuk, instead of writing: "His splendor was like the sunrise" (Habakkuk 3:4), had written: "His splendor was like the apparent movement of the Sun over the horizon due to the rotation of the Earth upon its axis." The latter may be more scientifically correct, but would it have communicated anything about the splendor of God? Would it even have had any meaning to someone who lived in the seventh century B.C.?

Why should we be so arrogant as to assume that if God had wanted to be completely scientific, we could understand him even today? Scientists are currently seeking one equation or set of equations describing the entire universe. If these equations were just given to us by God, would we have enough knowledge to understand them? Would we even be able to recognize them, or would we reject them as meaningless or possibly even wrong?

We might have a chance of understanding God's descriptions if they included a full mathematical proof. But then, we must remember that the Bible's purpose is not to teach science but to teach us about God.

A complete mathematical proof for such equations would be entirely out of place. Depending on the starting place and completeness of such a proof, it might even be longer than the entire Bible. While such proof might satisfy scientists today, what use would it have been to someone living thousands of years ago?

This brings us to the second problem, which concerns science. Unlike the Bible, with new information, science changes. Suppose we assume that the Bible is 100 percent correct and speaks on scientific issues. The changing nature of scientific thinking over the last 3000 years means conflicts between science and the Bible are inevitable. If the Bible deals with scientific issues, then for it to be scientifically correct today would mean that it conflicted with the "scientific" views when written.

Conflicts between science and Christianity during the 19th century caused many people, in and out of the church, to reject the Bible's reliability. Since then, many scientific theories that caused this rejection have been revised or discarded.

We have already seen this to be the case with archaeology, but other sciences have also made tremendous advances. Peter Stoner cites one such example in his book *Science Speaks*,

> On my desk I have Young's General Astronomy (1898). Many changes have taken place in astronomy since this was the standard college text of our country... Young's book is of relatively little value when it treats of things far from our solar system. Texts of astronomy two hundred years old are very entertaining, but in the light of present-day knowledge nearly everything is in error.[13]

If science is constantly changing, how could the Bible possibly be expected to agree with the scientific views of yesterday, today, and tomorrow? Quite simply, the only way the Bible would not conflict with science from time to time is if it does not deal with scientific issues.

---

13 Peter Stoner and R. C. Newman, *Science Speaks: Scientific Proof of the Accuracy of Prophecy and the Bible* (Chicago: Moody Press, 1968) pp. 7-8.

SCIENCE WITHOUT RELIGION?

Some see the differences between the natural and spiritual as a reason, in and of itself, to reject religion. Some believe religion was only a way to explain the natural world in ancient times. Thus, lightning resulted from a god who lived in the clouds and threw lightning bolts down to Earth.

When science comes along and provides a natural explanation for lightning, the god in the clouds is no longer needed. They claim religion is no longer needed because science has explained the natural world.

This argument has several problems, but a key one is that it has a false premise. This premise claims the primary function of religion is to explain the natural world. As we have already seen, religion is much more than this, if it even has that function.

Still, has science really explained the natural universe so completely that there is no room for God? Fundamentally, the explanations provided by science center around the concept of chance.

The general idea is that random forces came together and resulted in the universe – one aspect of which is you reading a book questioning whether all this occurred by chance. One area where chance fails as a reasonable explanation is life's origin.

Most scientists currently believe that chemical reactions in the seas of the young Earth produced the organic chemicals necessary for life. Over an extended period, these chemicals combined and recombined until this chemical evolution eventually resulted in life.

Scientists have even been able to duplicate the creation of amino acids, the primitive building blocks for life, using an experiment developed by Harold Urey and Stanley Miller in the 1950s. This experiment led some to conclude that the origin of life is a simple process. According to Charles Pellegrino and Jesse Stroff in their book *Darwin's Universe,*

> Life from nonlife. You could start the process in your own kitchen, if you wanted to. It's that easy. Assemble carbon, hydrogen, nitrogen, and oxygen in one

place... apply heat, shock waves, X-rays, or ultraviolet radiation... and invariably, within twenty hours or so, you
will have incited the formation of carbon compounds...
Yet such experiments involve only small volumes over
very short periods of time. What could be done with
entire oceans over a period of millions, or billions, of
years?[14]

The problem here is going from the amino acids to life itself is
a tremendous leap. It is a leap of such great magnitude that serious
questions exist as to whether or not it is even possible.

At first, scientists assumed the gap only seemed vast due to
our lack of understanding. They were confident that as we learned
more, we would discover that the gap was nowhere near as wide as
it appeared. At that point, the transition from chemical reactions
to life would be easier to understand.

Yet, as we learned more, that has not happened. On the contrary, rather than narrowing the gap, the more we learn, the wider
the gap becomes and the more impossible life seems to be.

Even the simplest forms of life are so complex that it is impossible to conceive how they could have come together by chance
alone. The earliest life would have had a similar complexity as a
simple bacterium. While simpler forms of life, such as viruses,
exist, they are parasites requiring more complex forms of life.

To make a simple bacterium requires approximately 2000 enzymes. Enzymes are collections of amino acids in a particular order
and structure. The structure of an enzyme allows it to accomplish
a particular task needed by the bacterium.

Since the number of amino acids and the structure of enzymes
are now known, we can calculate the odds of forming the enzymes
needed to create a single bacterium. The odds of obtaining a single
enzyme with the proper function is 1 chance in 10^{20} or a 1 followed
by 20 zeros. The odds for obtaining all 2000 enzymes needed to
create life would therefore be $(10^{20})^{2000}$, or only 1 chance in 10^{40000},
a 1 followed by 40,000 zeros.

---

14   Charles Pellegrino & Jesse Stroff, *Darwin's Universe: Origins and Crises in
the History of Life* (New York: Van Nostrand Reinhold, 1983) p. 106.

The number 10^{40000} is so large that it is beyond our comprehension. To give you some idea of just how small the odds are that all these enzymes could come together by chance, let's compare these odds to the chance of winning a lottery, where the odds of winning were 1 in 10^{40000}.

To improve your chances of winning, you could try to buy as many tickets as possible. Suppose you buy 100 trillion tickets every second for 100 trillion years, which is over 5000 times longer than the age of the universe given by scientists. You would have 3.16 X 10^{35} tickets. That is a lot of tickets, yet they would only increase your odds of winning to 1 chance in 3.17 X 10^{39964} or 317 followed by 39962 zeros. This number is impossibly large.

Things get even worse. We have only assembled the enzymes and have yet to assemble the bacterium. When we consider all the factors needed to assemble a simple bacterium, the odds reduce to an incredible 1 chance in $10^{100,000,000,000}$ or a 1 followed by 100 billion zeros.[15]

We can compare these odds to the maximum number of "chances" life on Earth could have had, estimated at 2.5 X 10^{51} even under the best conditions[16]. Thus, it is virtually impossible[17] for life to emerge simply by chance alone. Robert Shapiro, professor of Chemistry and an expert on DNA research, has said of these odds,

> The improbability involved in generating even one bacterium is so large that it reduces all considerations of time and space to nothingness. Given such odds, the time until the black holes evaporate and the space to the ends of the universe would make no difference at

---

15 Robert Shapiro, *Origins: A Skeptic's Guide to the Creation of Life on Earth* (New York: Summit Books, 1986) pp. 127-8.

16 Robert Shapiro, Origins: A Skeptic's Guide to the Creation of Life on Earth (New York: Summit Books, 1986) pp. 126.

17 While it is true that even with these odds there is a very small chance for the spontaneous origin of life, it must also be conceded that if one does not consider odds of 1 chance in $10^{100,000,000,000}$ as impossible, then truly nothing is impossible. One must ask however, which requires more faith: God or random chance?.

all. If we were to wait, we would truly be waiting for a miracle.[18]

Suppose one is to maintain a belief in chemical evolution leading to life. There must have been some intermediate stages between amino acids and enzymes. But any intermediate stage, any sort of pre-enzyme, would have been inherently unstable. Such a stage would have broken down into amino acids before progressing to the next intermediate stage. There are lower limits to the complexity of a cell below which you cannot go.

Many see a potential solution to these problems in the theory of an "RNA world" because of the RNA molecule's potential to be self-replicating. But many problems remain, with the creation of the first RNA molecule, and then going from an RNA molecule to a simple living cell.

It is as if you were trying to explain the origin of the airplane by natural means. One could discard the radar and autopilot as nonessential components. You could toss the radio as a later adaptation. The body could be open, and the controls simplified. Still, one eventually comes to a lower limit. Remove the wings, and you no longer have a functioning plane. Even the simplest cell is vastly more complex than an airplane.

This concept has been more rigorously refined by Michael Behe as *irreducible complexity*, which he defines as,

> a single system composed of several well-matched, interacting parts that contribute to the basic function, wherein the removal of any one of the parts causes the system to effectively cease functioning. An irreducibly complex system cannot be produced directly (that is, by continuously improving the initial function, which continues to work by the same mechanism) by slight, successive modifications of a precursor system, because any precursor to the irreducibly complex system that is missing a part is by definition nonfunctional.[19]

---

18 Robert Shapiro, Origins: A Skeptic's Guide to the Creation of Life on Earth (New York: Summit Books, 1986) pp. 128.

19 Michael Behe, *Darwin's Black Box: The Biochemical Challenge to Evolution* (New York: The Free Press, 1996) pp. 39.

The more scientists investigate the origin of life on Earth, the more improbable it gets. Behe points out that,

> The simplicity that was once expected to be the foundation of life has proven to be a phantom; instead, systems of horrendous, irreducible complexity inhabit the cell.[20]

Recent studies have further compounded the problems by indicating that the assumptions concerning the early atmosphere were overly optimistic. As it turns out, the early atmosphere was not very conducive to the origin of life and may have been hostile.[21]

To top it off, it turns out that there was nowhere near as much time available as scientists once thought. Rather than over a billion years to evolve life, scientists have found that life was on the Earth only about 170 million years after the crust cooled.

Why is it still accepted if the odds are so great against the origin of life by chance? Many scientists ignore the difficulties. They assume that despite the problems, that life not only must arise naturally but that it must have been an easy process! Pellegrino and Stroff, considering the origin of DNA, state that,

> It could not have been impossible. It could not even have been very unlikely, because it is here. And it has been here for at least 3.5 billion years.[22]

Andrew Scott pointed out another reason in his book, *The Creation of Life*, when he stated,

---

20   Michael Behe, *Darwin's Black Box: The Biochemical Challenge to Evolution* (New York: The Free Press, 1996) pp. 252.

21   Fred Hoyle & N C Wickramasinghe, Lifecloud: The Origin of Life in the Universe (New York: Harper and Row, 1978) pp. 25-6.
     Michael Denton, Evolution, A Theory in Crisis (Bethesda, Maryland: Adler & Adler, 1985) pp. 260-3.
     Robert Shapiro, Origins: A Skeptic's Guide to the Creation of Life on Earth (New York: Summit Books, 1986) pp. 111-2
     C. Thaxton, W. Bradley and R. Olsen, *The Mystery of Life's Origin* (New York: Philosophical Library, 1984) pp. 69-94.

22   Charles Pellegrino & Jesse Stroff, *Darwin's Universe: Origins and Crises in the History of Life* (New York: Van Nostrand Reinhold, 1983) p. 71.

> Most scientists *want* to believe that life could have emerged spontaneously from the primeval waters, because it would confirm their belief in the explicability of Nature... They also want to believe because their arch opponents – religious fundamentalists such as creationists – *do not* believe in life's spontaneous origin. It is this combative atmosphere which sometimes encourages scientists writing and speaking about the origin of life to become as dogmatic and bigoted as the creationist opponents they so despise.[23]

Because of the difficulty with the origin of life, some scientists have concluded that life could not have originated here on Earth. Perhaps the most famous of these are Fred Hoyle and Chandra Wickramasinghe. According to Wickramasinghe,

> The organic soup itself is not such a marvelous thing. It is a prerequisite for any biological activity to start; that's certainly true. But it doesn't follow that if you have an organic soup it could get life started... when we looked at the probabilities of the assembly of organic materials into a living system, it turns out that the improbabilities are really horrendous, horrific in extent and I concluded along with my colleague that (this) could not have happened spontaneously on the Earth. There's not enough time, there's not enough resources and there's no way in which that could have happened on the Earth.[24]

Where did life come from if life did not originate here on Earth? According to Hoyle and Wickramasinghe,

> The best explanation therefore of the known facts relating to the origin of life on the Earth is that in the early days soft landing of comets brought about the spreading of water and other volatiles over the Earth's surface. Then about four billion years ago life also arrived from a life-bearing comet.[25]

---

23 Andrew Scott, *The Creation of Life: Past, Future, Alien* (New York: Basil Blackwell, 1986) pp. 111-12.

24 Chandra Wickramasinghe, *Science and the Divine Origin of Life* in *Intellectuals Speak Out About God* ed. Roy Abraham Varghese (Dallas, Texas: Lewis and Stanley 1984) pp. 25-6.

25 Fred Hoyle & N C Wickramasinghe, *Lifecloud: The Origin of Life in the Universe* (New York: Harper and Row, 1978) p. 134.

Yet, this only shifts the problem; it does not eliminate it. The problem becomes: How did life begin in space? It does allow more time for chemical evolution to create life. Still, the increase is insignificant compared to the amount of time needed.

In reality, this is just a way to sweep the problem under the carpet and ignore it. In 1981, Francis Crick, who won the Nobel Prize for his role in the discovery of the DNA molecule, wrote,

> An honest man, armed with all the knowledge available to us now, could only state that in some sense, the origin of life appears at the moment to be almost a miracle, so many are the conditions which would have to have been satisfied to get it going.[26]

The idea that life emerged by chance is nothing more than a modern scientific myth.[27] While one may believe it, as many scientists have recently pointed out, there is very little evidence to support it and lots of evidence against it. It is not the evidence that leads to this conclusion but the fundamental presupposition.

ONLY A MATTER OF TIME?

The odds against life occurring by chance alone are incredibly large. But then, most scientists believe that there was lots of time for chance to operate. Often these odds are ignored with the argument that given enough time, even the most unlikely event must happen. There are two problems with this line of reasoning.

One of these is a pervasive problem affecting many people, especially in casinos. This problem is the Gambler's Fallacy. The Gambler's Fallacy can be summed up in the phrase, "if I play long enough, my number has to come up."

This reasoning is flawed. The odds of an event occurring do not improve with time. Even if given an infinite amount of time,

---

26   Francis Crick, *Life Itself* (New York: Simon and Schuster, 1981) p. 88.
27   Robert Shapiro, *Origins: A Skeptic's Guide to the Creation of Life on Earth* (New York: Summit Books, 1986) pp. 33, 301.
     Fred Hoyle & N C Wickramasinghe, *Lifecloud: The Origin of Life in the Universe* (New York: Harper and Row, 1978) p. 26.

the chances against life just happening, remain just as astronomi-
cally large and impossible.

The second problem is that the more scientists discover about
the natural world, the more unlikely it is that the world could have
come about by chance. Even the laws of nature themselves show a
structure that calls into question the idea of chance.

In the process of understanding the universe, scientists have
discovered many physical constants and parameters. Recently,
many scientists have pointed out that if the universe is to contain
life, the values of these parameters are incredibly critical.

For example, one of the four fundamental forces in nature is
the strong nuclear force. This force is responsible for holding the
nucleus of an atom (the protons and neutrons) together. If this
force were just a few percent stronger, then all of the hydrogen in
the universe would have combined into helium. Without hydrogen, you cannot have life.

On the other hand, if the strong nuclear force had been just
a few percent weaker, it would not have been strong enough to
hold together the larger atoms, such as carbon. Again life would
not have been possible.

Another critical parameter is the mass of the universe. Often
I have heard people use the size of the universe as an argument
against God. Why would God have created such a large universe
with billions of galaxies yet be concerned with only us? While this
argument has several problems, there is a scientific answer as to
why the universe is so large.

Imagine a smaller universe, one with less mass. In that case,
there would not have been enough helium produced during the
early period of the Big Bang to create the heavier elements needed for life. Conversely, imagining a universe with a larger mass,
then you have too much deuterium created. Too much deuterium
would have caused the stars to burn much more rapidly, and they
would have burned out before there was enough time for the development of life.

Another problem with a smaller universe would have been with the amount of time it existed. The special theory of relativity, discovered by Einstein during the early twentieth century, linked the concepts of space and time. Because of this, if you know the size of the universe, then you can determine how long it will last. As John Barrow and Frank Tipler described the problem in their book, *The Anthropic Cosmological Principle,*

> If our Universe were to contain just a single galaxy like the Milky Way, containing 10^{11} stars, instead of 10_{12} such galaxies, we might regard this a sensible cosmic economy with little consequence for life. But, a universe of mass $10^{11}M_0$ [M_0 = Solar Mass] would. . . have expanded for only about a month. No observers could have evolved to witness such an economy-sized universe.[28]

The universe is the size it is because it needs to be this size to support life.

There are many other parameters, such as these. Many are extremely critical. For instance, maintaining stars like our Sun requires an incredible balancing act between the forces of gravity and electromagnetism. Vary either of these forces by more than 1 part in 10^{40}, a 1 followed by 40 zeros, and our Sun could not exist.[29] One part in 10^{40} is equivalent to the mass of one paperclip compared to the mass of 10 million stars like our Sun.

So many parameters observed in nature show this preference for life that many scientists have begun to take note. As the physicist Stephen Hawking wrote:

> The laws of science, as we know them at present, contain many fundamental numbers, like the size of the electric charge of the electron and the ratio of the masses of the proton and the electron... The remarkable fact is that the values of these numbers seem to have

---

28 John Barrow & Frank Tipler, *The Anthropic Cosmological Principle* (Oxford: Clarendon Press, 1986) p. 385.

29 Roy Peacock, *A Brief History of Eternity* (Wheaton, IL: Crossway Books, 1990) p. 120.

been very finely adjusted to make possible the development of life.[30]

As a result, scientists have begun to talk about the Anthropic
Principle, which Hawking defined as, "We see the universe the way
it is because if it were different, we would not be here to observe
it."[31] We can also define this concept as the universe exists this way
to support human life!

The anthropic principle is, in reality, science confirming the
Teleological Argument for the existence of God. The eighteenth-cen-
tury clergyman William Paley best summarized the teleological
argument.

According to Paley, suppose you were walking along a deserted
island beach and came across a complex watch lying in the sand.
From its design and structure, you would conclude that a watch-
maker must have existed, and such a finely tuned object could not
have come about through chance alone.

Scientists have discovered that the natural universe is much
more finely tuned than any watch. It would seem to have been
created with the specific purpose of supporting life. Astronomer
Robert Jastrow summarized the current situation,

> Thus, according to the physicist and the astron-
> omer, it appears that the Universe was constructed
> within very narrow limits, in such a way that man could
> dwell in it. This result is called the *anthropic principle*. It
> is the most theistic result ever to come out of science,
> in my view.[32]

A common objection to this line of reasoning is that this is
simply a God-of-the-gaps argument. But such criticisms oversim-
plify the argument and thus somewhat miss the point.

---

30 Stephen Hawking, *A Brief History of Time: From the Big Bang to Black
    Holes* (New York: Bantam Books, 1988) p. 125.

31 Stephen Hawking, *A Brief History of Time: From the Big Bang to Black
    Holes* (New York: Bantam Books, 1988) p. 183.

32 Robert Jastrow, *The Astronomer and God* in *The Intellectuals Speak Out
    About God* ed. Roy Abraham Varghese.

The claim here is not a God-of-the-gaps argument, which essentially says, 'we do not know; therefore, God must have done it.' Instead, this is an argument based on evidence that points to design and a designer.

Some have tried to claim that, by definition, science cannot point to a designer. Science deals with natural phenomena such as the motion of the planets or why earthquakes happen. Issues of design are beyond the scope of science. Yet this is not entirely true. The issue of design plays a significant role in anthropology. There, scientists try to determine, for example, if the shape of a rock was the result of nature or shaped and designed to make it a tool.

The work of William Dembski has made some strides in understanding the criteria for design. These center around the concept of 'specified complexity.' Two aspects must be satisfied to have specified complexity that points to design. One is that the thing under consideration must be highly improbable; the other is that it must fit some identifiable pattern. As Dembski states,

> Complexity guarantees, that the object in question is not so simple that it can readily be attributed to chance. Specification guarantees that the object exhibits the right sort of pattern associated with intelligent causes. A single letter of the alphabet is specified without being complex, a long sequence of random numbers is complex without being specified. A Shakespearean sonnet is both complex and specified. *Specified complexity* is how we detect design empirically.[33]

The argument here is not that science has not figured it out; therefore, God must have done it. Instead, the origin of life is so complex and specified that it points to a designer. If one allows that it is at least a possibility that God does exist and that He created life, does not the evidence of specified complexity point to this?

From what we know, it seems impossible for life to have arisen simply by chance, and it shows signs of design. Is it scientific to have faith that someday, despite the current evidence against it, we will find a natural explanation that does not require a designer?

---

33 William A. Dembski, Intelligent Design: The Bridge Between Science & Theology (Downers Grove, Illinois: InterVarsity Press, 1999) p. 17.

It would seem that the evidence, rather than eliminating the need for God, now points to a Creator who designed the universe to support life.

CONCLUSION

One must be careful when comparing science and Christianity. Science deals only with the natural world, while Christianity deals with the relationship between God and His creation. While science can help us learn about how the universe operates, Christianity can help us learn about our relationship with our Creator.

Many advances in modern science point to the existence of a God who designed the universe to support life. Henry Margenau, Professor of Physics at Yale and former editor of the *American Journal of Science, Philosophy of Science,* and *Review of Modern Physics,* when asked about the hostility to religion that supposedly exists among scientists, responded,

> Well, this is a common belief. And, if you ask scientists who have a mild training in science, especially high school teachers and so forth, you do get the impression that there is a conflict between science and religion. But if you ask really good scientists, I mean men who have made contributions, I'm thinking of people here like Eccles, like Wigner, who is a good friend of mine, Heisenberg, whom I personally knew, Schroedinger, who visited me personally at home... Einstein was less explicit about his religious views, but he had it. The leading scientists, the people who have made the contributions which has made science grow so vastly in the last fifty years, are, so far as I know, all religious in their beliefs. None of these men had any objection to religion... All these men were intensely interested in religion.[34]

When we consider the proper relationship between science and religion, the natural versus the spiritual, we find no inherent conflict. Just because there need not be a conflict does not mean that a conflict does not exist. In the next chapter, we will examine

34 Henry Margenau, *Modern Physics and the Turn to Belief in God* in *The Intellectuals Speak out About God* ed. by Roy Abraham Varghese (Dallas, Texas: Lewis and Stanley, 1984) pp. 43-4.

some of the Bible's statements concerning the natural world to see how these assertions conform to the current findings of modern science.

5

SCIENCE AND THE BIBLE

*Most of the scientific "errors" that critics claim to have
found in the Bible involves its alleged miracles.
(Henry Morris)*[1]

THE CONFLICT BETWEEN SCIENCE AND THE BIBLE during the nineteenth century led many to reject the Bible and to support liberal theories concerning its development. While many scientific findings forming the basis of this rejection have since been significantly revised or even rejected, this attitude concerning the Bible persists.

Today, many believe that while it may have been possible for an educated person to accept the Bible as the word of God 200 years ago, since that time, science has shown the Bible to be in error in many places. A case in point involves the astronomer Robert Jastrow.

While, as we pointed out in the last chapter, he accepts that the universe had a beginning and quite possibly a Creator, Jastrow believes that,

> science and religion only agree on the necessity of a Beginning; science disagrees with the Bible about most other things that occurred in the history of the Universe after the Beginning.[2]

As we saw in the last chapter, science and the Bible deal with different subjects. Science is concerned with the natural, and the

---

1   Henry M Morris, *Science and the Bible* (Chicago: Moody Press, 1986) p. 25.
2   Robert Jastrow, *The Intellectuals Speak Out About God* ed. Roy Abraham Varghese (Dallas, Texas: Lewis and Stanley, 1984) p. 18.

Bible the spiritual. We should not expect to either prove or disprove the Bible with science.

Does this mean we can say nothing concerning the Bible from a scientific point of view? Are the two subjects so utterly different that they never intersect? No, there are places where science deals with the same subjects as the Bible. So with the limitations mentioned in the last chapter in mind, let us look at a fundamental subject dealt with directly by both the Bible and science – the existence of the universe.

CREATION

The Bible's position on the existence of the universe is very clear. It teaches that, at some point, God created the universe. The Bible opens with "In the beginning God created the heavens and the earth" (Genesis 1:1). This creation was not organizing existing matter into its present form, but a creation out of nothing. The writer of the book of Hebrews tells us, "the universe was formed at God's command, so that what is seen was not made out of what was visible" (Hebrews 11:3).

As a matter of pure chance, the Bible should have a fifty-fifty chance of being correct. Either the universe had a beginning or has always existed in one form or another. With only two choices, one has to be correct.

Science has taken both positions. At the beginning of the scientific revolution, most scientists generally accepted a universe created by God.[3] During the nineteenth century, many questioned traditional religious views, and rationalism was the new religion.[4]

---

3   As we saw in the last chapter, the concept of explaining something by referring to the actions of an intelligent being is not unscientific. An archaeologist uncovering a bowl, for example, would not try to explain the existence of the bowl by natural means, but would conclude it had been made by someone. This would be a valid scientific conclusion.

4   See Elgin Hushbeck, *Secularism and Christianity: Consider Christianity Volume 2* (Gonzalez, Florida, Energion) Chapter 1.

Since rationalism rejects upfront any sort of supernatural explanation, those following it rejected the idea of a God creating the universe. Since it would have been impossible for the universe to have created itself, the ideal of a static, unchanging universe became the accepted scientific explanation.

To the scientists of the nineteenth and early twentieth centuries, the universe exists as it does because it has always existed this way. The universe does not change. If you could enter a time machine and travel through time, no matter which way or how far you went, the universe, as a whole, would look essentially the same.

Things might change on a smaller level; individual stars will be born out of the stellar dust, grow old and die, only to be reborn again as new stars. Still, overall, the universe would look pretty much the same as it does now.

Scientists accepted this idea of a static universe up until the 1920s. By that time, it was becoming apparent that a static universe did not fit very well into the new theory of relativity. For the universe to remain static required a virtually impossible balancing act in which any movement would set off a process of either expansion or contraction.

In 1929, Edwin Hubble, working at Mount Wilson Observatory in California, destroyed what remained of the static universe theory when he discovered what is now called the Hubble Law of Recession.

One way astronomers study stars is by breaking down the light they give off into their component parts. The result is called a spectrogram, a series of lines, something like an extended bar code in which each line represents a different wavelength of light. In the spectrogram of stars, these lines are not distributed randomly but fall into identifiable patterns. It is by these patterns that stars can be classified.

The spectrogram of a star is affected by the relative movement of that star to the Earth. Just as the sound of a jet will change as it approaches, passes overhead, and then flies away, the color of a star's light also changes depending on whether it is moving toward or away. This change is called a doppler shift.

Because of the doppler shift, a star moving toward us appears to emit light at a higher frequency than it actually does. As a result, the pattern of lines making up its spectrogram shifts toward the high-frequency end of the spectrum.

The high-frequency part of the visible spectrum is composed of blue light. So a star approaching us is said to have a *blue shift*. The reverse is true for a star that is moving away, and its light would appear to have a lower frequency than it actually does. Since the low-frequency part of the visible spectrum is composed of red light, a star moving away is said to have a *red shift*.

Hubble discovered, and other astronomers confirmed, that nearly all galaxies have a red shift and are thus all moving away from us. Hubble also noticed a relationship between the distance of a galaxy and the amount of the shift. The further the galaxy, the more the light was shifted, and thus the faster it was moving away from us. This relationship between the red shift and distance is the Hubble Law of Recession. It showed that we do not live in a static universe but one that is expanding.

An expanding universe has tremendous implications regarding the question of creation. If the universe is expanding, it must be larger now than it was in the past. Consequently, the further back in time we look, the smaller the universe. If we look far enough back, the entire universe would be contained in a tiny point.

It is impossible to determine a particular fixed point in space from which the universe started, and to try is to misunderstand what happened. Not only are the galaxies moving away from each other, but the space that contains the galaxies is expanding. There was no particular fixed point in space where the universe started. The entire universe was contained in a single point. From this one point, known as a singularity, the universe began in an explosion of incomprehensible magnitude: the Big Bang.

THE BIG BANG

The Big Bang Theory brought scientists back to what was, for many of them, an unsettling conclusion: that there may have been a creation after all. Stephen Hawking, perhaps the most significant theoretical physicist since Einstein, wrote the following concerning the implications of the Big Bang,

> Many people do not like the idea that time had a beginning, probably because it smacks of divine intervention... There were therefore a number of attempts to avoid the conclusion that there had been a big bang.[5]

At first, many scientists rejected the idea of the Big Bang. After all, the earliest estimates showed the Big Bang occurring *after* the formation of the Earth – a definite problem. Still, since the 1950s, the theory has enjoyed growing support.

Since then, observational evidence has strongly supported the Big Bang, most notably the 1965 discovery of background radiation believed remnants of the fireball created by the explosion. Today the Big Bang Theory is accepted by the vast majority of scientists.

With the experimental result over the last few decades, the debate moved past whether there was a Big Bang. It has largely moved past what type of Big Bang since the consensus is that it was an inflationary Big Bang. Today the discussion has moved on to further refinements of the theory, such as the universe's shape.[6]

Over the last several decades, scientists have returned to an acceptance that, while they may not call it creation, the natural universe did have a beginning. Scientists now believe they can describe the events that took place right after the explosion to a surprising degree of accuracy. They even talk of events one-millionth of a second after the Big Bang.

---

5   Stephen W. Hawking, *A Brief History of Time, From the Big Bang to Black Holes* (New York: Bantam Books, 1988) pp. 46-7.

6   Brian Greene, *The Fabric f the Cosmos* (New York: Knoph, 2004) pp. 251- 303.

While marking the universe's beginning, the Big Bang is, at least for now, a stop sign to science. Science can approach the Big Bang but can go no further. This stop sign is because the Big Bang is literally the beginning of the natural universe as we know it. One cannot talk of a time before the Big Bang since everything we know of, including time itself, started with this explosion.

There was nothing, and then suddenly, there was the universe. How did the universe come to be? Why did the Big Bang explode? Why did the universe form the way that it did? These are questions that science may not be able to answer. Stephen Hawking said, concerning the origins of the universe,

> The odds against a universe like ours emerging out of something like the Big Bang are enormous... I think there are clearly religious implications whenever you start to discuss the origins of the universe. There must be religious overtones. But I think most scientists prefer to shy away from the religious side of it.[7]

Even after the evidence for the Big Bang, and thus a beginning became too strong to ignore, scientists still sought ways to avoid any hint such a beginning might point to a creator.

I want to be clear this is not a criticism of scientists. After all, since science deals with the natural world, it is good and proper that they seek natural explanations wherever possible. This is expected when looking at this issue from a scientific point of view.

However, there is a critical distinction in terms of the question here. On the one hand, are tested theories; on the other, there are the proposed theories and speculations. Since the Big Bang theory became a settled issue among scientists, the settled parts are either consistent with or supportive of the idea that there was a creator. The current speculations sought ways to avoid this conclusion.

For example, an early attempt to avoid a beginning suggested that perhaps the universe oscillates. The universe explodes and expands out until gravity slows the expanding matter down and

---

7   John Boslough, *Stephen Hawking's Universe, An Introduction to the Most Remarkable Scientist of Our Time* (New York: William Morrow & Co; 1985) p. 121

pulls it back together. This collapse forms a new singularity for a new Big Bang.

The pull of gravity is related to the amount of matter: the more matter, the stronger the pull. A problem with this theory was the early evidence showed there was not enough matter to stop the expansion and pull everything back in so it could expand again. Calculations show that there was a considerable gap.

There were other problems as well. Even if scientists found enough matter to stop the expansion and showed the universe would collapse in the distant future, this would still leave the question of why the initial explosion occurred in the first place. Harry L. Shipman of the University of Delaware described what might happen if the universe were to collapse again,

> The galaxies will start approaching each other again, will coalesce, and will approach a time when the universe looks as it did at the beginning, a dense blob. What happens next? Our view is limited. We cannot guess what happens at this time... We scientists can speculate about what will happen, but when we speculate in this way we are leaving the territory of science and are trespassing on the territory of the philosopher and the theologian.[8]

This situation is where things stood for the first edition of this book. Since then, investigations in the 1990s have moved this issue from speculation to settled.

One way scientists could answer this question is to measure the deceleration rate. If the universe's expansion were slowing fast enough, it would eventually stop and collapse. Seeking to measure the deceleration rate of the universe, separate studies conducted by Saul Perlmutter and Brian Schmidt reached the same and very surprising conclusion. Not only is the universe's expansion not slowing down enough to result in a collapse, but it is accelerating! The universe is not oscillating in an endless series of big bangs, as scientists once thought.

---

8   Harry L. Shipman, *Black Holes, Quasars, & the Universe* (Boston Mass: Houghton Miffen Co, 1976) p. 238.

Still, science has not, nor should it, stop here, and scientists continue to speculate and theorize about the universe's origin. The details of this go well beyond the scope of this book, and for those interested, Brian Greene's recent book, *The Fabric of the Cosmos,* would be a great place to start.

As it currently stands, there are two major competing theories on the origin of the universe. The inflationary Big Bang model explains much of the universe around us. Yet, at least in a natural sense, it is hard to explain how it started.

The other is the cyclic model, which is a new twist on the oscillating universe theory based on the findings of quantum mechanics. It also solves a lot of problems and additionally takes into account the theories of quantum mechanics.

However, while it oscillates, these would eventually wind down; thus, the oscillations would not go on indefinitely. As a result, this theory also suffers from the problem of how the process started in the first place.[9]

During the updating for the third edition, many stories and YouTube videos claimed the recently launched James Webb Space Telescope (JWST) had proven the Big Bang did not happen. While sensational news, these stories were not entirely correct. The Big Bang theory is not a single theory but a group of similar theories, each trying to explain the origin and development of the universe.

As with all scientific theories, new evidence leads to further refinements. The early results from the JWST did show that some early galaxies were more developed than some Big Bang theories had expected. Still, this is far from showing the Big Bang did not happen.[10]

So the evidence is that the universe had a beginning. While there are always speculations and theories, if we accept the principle

---

9   Brian Greene, *The Fabric of the Cosmos* (New York: Knoph, 2004) p. 410-412.

10   Jackson Ryan, *No, James Webb Space Telescope Images do not Debunk the Big Bang* CNET Science, Aug 22,2022, https://www.cnet.com/science/space/ no-james-webb-space-telescope-images-do-not-debunk-the-big-bang/.

that actions have causes, which is one of the foundations of science, the question becomes: What or who caused the Big Bang?

Given this, is it irrational to consider that at least one of the possible options is a concept of God? Carl Sagan, in his book *Cosmos*, addresses this question as follows,

> Was there a tiny universe, devoid of all matter, and then the matter suddenly created from nothing? How does *that* happen? In many cultures it is customary to answer that God created the universe out of nothing. But this is mere temporizing. If we wish courageously to pursue the question, we must, of course ask next where God comes from. And if we decide this to be unanswerable, why not save a step and decide that the origin of the universe is an unanswerable question? Or, if we say that God has always existed, why not save a step and conclude that the universe has always existed?[11]

The Big Bang theory presents us with the problem of creation out of nothing without a cause. One obvious solution would be that God caused the Big Bang. While acknowledging this solution, Sagan believes we should instead "save a step," concluding the question is either unanswerable or the universe has always existed. But there are a few problems with Sagan's suggestions.

Sagan's first suggestion that we declare the problem unanswerable is hardly a solution. This is nothing more than ignoring the problem, hoping it will disappear. His other suggestion is to declare the universe to be eternal. Scientists believed in this solution in the nineteenth century, before the discovery of an expanding universe and the Big Bang.

You could justify this solution as little as forty years ago. Still, the current evidence calls this into question. The universe has not always existed but began at a certain point. In addition, the concept of an eternal universe based on cause and effect is logically impossible.[12] Continuing to hold that the universe is eternal is grounded more in faith. The evidence points to a beginning.

---

11 Carl Sagan, *Cosmos* (New York: Random House, 1980) p. 257.

12 An infinite series of causes and effect would never complete, even if given and infinite amount of time. If the universe had always existed, it would be the result of an infinite series of causes and effect. For

Consequently, both of Sagan's suggestions are, in essence, that we ignore the problem rather than accept the conclusion to which the evidence points – a universe created by God. Sagan claims this is justified because appealing to God as the Creator "is mere temporizing." If we don't ignore these problems with the universe, we will have to face them when it comes to God. Thus he suggests that we "*save a step.*"

There is a principle of reason called Occam's razor, stating we should reject unnecessarily complex explanations in favor of simpler ones. Still, it does not apply here because you do not have the same problems with an eternal God that you do with an eternal universe.

From a Christian perspective, "Where did God come from?" is answered in scripture. "From everlasting to everlasting," God has existed (Psalm 90:2). God is not governed by cause and effect in the same way the universe is. Since time is part of the universe, as the Creator of the universe, He exists apart from time as we know it.

Put simply, God, by definition, is eternal, while the universe is not. Appealing to God as the Creator of the universe is not "mere temporizing" but a solution. One may not like the solution or its implications. Still, it is a solution and one that is consistent with the evidence.

Is it possible to accept the creation and still reject the Creator? Of course, all one needs to do is ignore the implications of the creation. After all, this is not scientific proof for God because, by definition, science can only take us up to the Big Bang.

In fact, many would consider an affirmative answer to the question "Did God create the universe?" inherently unscientific. Science can point to the universe having a beginning and a designer. As we saw in the last chapter, there is a lot of evidence to support this view. But identifying this designer with God would be, strictly speaking, outside the scope of science.

---

more information see the discussion on the Cosmological argument in *Christianity and Secularism, Consider Christianity Series, Volume 2.*

For many, even the conclusion that the evidence points to a designer is too religious. In their view, such a conclusion cannot be scientific. If science cannot answer this question by its very nature, then while we can use science to help guide our search, we cannot rely totally on science for an answer.

This conclusion is an essential concept, for some claim that science is the only source of truth. For those who hold such a position, the fact that science restricts its investigation to the natural is reason enough to conclude that only the natural world exists. Still, as we pointed out in the last chapter, such a position is self-refuting.

However, there is another problem with this position: it is irrational to seek an answer from a source incapable of giving all possible answers should they be true.

For example, say you had a machine that could give you the correct answer to almost any question, as long as the answer was 'yes' or 'no.' But there was a problem, for in one area, say, questions dealing with dogs, the machine had a flaw, and as a result, the machine could only answer no to those questions.

In such a case, would it be rational to seek an answer from the machine concerning dogs? Given that the machine will always say no to such questions, would it tell you anything useful? Of course not! If science cannot answer "yes" to the question, "Did God create the universe" then is it reasonable to seek this answer from science?

A QUESTION OF TIME

There is another problem with the whole discussion of the creation of the universe. The problem is that when you get back to the very beginning, things become so foreign that they are challenging to discuss. When scientists talk about the Big Bang, they are not just talking about the origin of galaxies, stars, and planets; they are also talking about space, time, and even the laws of nature.

You can see the problems in the question, "What caused the Big Bang?" Usually, the answer to such a question would refer to something before the Big Bang. Yet the meaning of the word 'before' is bound up with the concept of time. But what does "before" mean if time did not exist, as time was created in the Big Bang?

Another problem involves the whole concept of the terms natural and supernatural. Many scientists are uncomfortable with a beginning, seeking an eternal universe. Be it the early static universe or the more recent cyclic universe theories, a beginning opens the possibility of a non-natural explanation. In contrast, an eternal universe can be completely natural.

The term 'natural' was historically the reality of space and time governed by natural laws in which we live. The supernatural was another reality beyond our reality, not governed by space, time, and natural laws like we are.

But what does this mean when we begin talking about the universe's origin? Everything we would typically think of as natural came into existence in this origin. So, what does that make the reality that caused the universe?

Science is constantly changing. As we have seen, scientists have already moved from accepting a divine creation to rejecting a creation altogether. They have now come back to accepting at least a beginning, though they still seek a way to avoid the implications of this.

It is possible that in the future, scientists will once again find a way to reject the belief in an origin. Yet, who is to say that fifty years after that, another discovery might lead them to accept an origin again?

This change is one of the reasons it is essential to distinguish between what is current speculation and what are supported theories. It is always easy to speculate God is no longer needed, especially when the basis is an untested proposal. After all, in just the years since the first edition of this book, things changed such that this section required significant updating.

THE HEAT OF THE MOMENT

Given this conclusion, it is hard to see how some can be so sure that science has eliminated the need for God, especially considering the other problems with an eternally existing universe. As we said above, an eternal universe is logically impossible. Still, there are scientific problems, and one of the most fundamental of these problems is the Second Law of Thermodynamics.

The Second Law of Thermodynamics states that closed systems eventually reach a state of disorganization. Put simply: they run down. A wristwatch will only keep working for a finite period until it uses all of its energy. One must periodically add more energy to the watch to keep it running by winding it or replacing the battery. The energy used to run the watch is lost and cannot be reused. If this were not the case, it would be possible to build a watch, or for that matter a car, that would power itself.

Another illustration of the Second Law of Thermodynamics is life on Earth. The Earth is a planet full of life. Life uses energy, so life on Earth must have an energy source to function. The primary source of energy for Earth is the Sun.

Yet, of all the energy given off by the Sun, only a tiny fraction ever hits the Earth, and life uses only a small fraction. Most energy the Sun generates goes into space before life can use it. The small fraction of energy life uses is also lost. Eventually, the Sun will use up its energy, and all life on Earth will cease to exist.[13]

The Second Law of Thermodynamics states that the amount of usable energy continually decreases. Because of this decrease, closed systems need an external energy source to continue operating, just as life on earth needing the Sun.

Applying the Second Law of Thermodynamics to the universe as a whole, one quickly realizes that the universe must have had a beginning simply because it has not run down yet. If the universe had existed forever, then the amount of usable energy in the uni-

---

13 Actually, all life will end before this point because before the Sun runs out of fuel it will expand and engulf the Earth.

verse, no matter how large, would already have been used up. The universe would not have the usable energy left to sustain life, and we would not exist.

This problem occurs with the most recent version of the cyclic universe theory. Each time the universe collapsed and exploded, it would lose some energy. Therefore, it could not cycle forever. Since we are obviously here, the universe has not yet run down. It either has a beginning or receives energy from an external source. In either case, there is still a place for a creator.

When looking at the question, *did God create the universe*, all of these issues come into play, and the conclusions one draws depend on many things. How one defines terms such as natural and supernatural? How one sees the role of science will strongly affect how one evaluates the evidence.

In our day-to-day lives, these issues are rarely a problem. Still, as one considers the beginning of the universe, the laws of nature and many of our concepts of reality break down. We can say that the evidence is consistent with the idea of a creator and gives considerable support to that view. Still, this is just the first step, and we have not shown the biblical account is correct. After all, there are still questions about the sequence of events and the time involved.

IN THE BEGINNING...

The question of the sequence of events reflects the problem mentioned in the last chapter regarding extracting scientific information from the Bible. Examining the creation account in Genesis will show that its primary purpose was to demonstrate our relationship with the rest of creation and God.

In this goal, the Genesis account succeeds beautifully. As a technical description of the world's creation, it leaves much to be desired, but this was not its purpose. If God had wanted to tell us *how* He created the world, it would have been a little longer than two chapters.

Even if we try to look to Genesis accounts for a scientific description of creation, the details given concerning the actual mechanics of the creation are sketchy enough that one can see them fitting or not fitting, depending on your intent, many possible scenarios. Some have claimed that the description given in Genesis 1 is full of errors. According to Isaac Asimov,

> any real comparison between what the Bible says and what the astronomer thinks shows us instantly that the two have virtually nothing in common.[14]

So let's briefly look at the events recorded in the first chapter of Genesis to see if they conflict with modern science or can be reconciled.[15] The first two verses of Genesis set the framework for the description that follows, (Note: the superscript numbers are the verse numbers.)

> [1]In the beginning God created the heavens and the earth. [2]Now the earth was formless and empty, darkness was over the surface of the deep, and the Spirit of God was hovering over the water. (Genesis 1:1-2)

The first verse covers the creation of the entire universe, from what we would now call the Big Bang up to the formation of the Earth. In verse two, we see that we are now only concerned with the Earth and that our point of view is from the planet's surface. By this time, water covers the planet's surface, and the earth is shrouded in darkness, most likely from a thick cloud cover.

The following 11 verses describe the appearance of light (thinning of the clouds), the separation of the waters from the waters (development of a water cycle needed to support life), the emergence of dry land, and the emergence of plant life.

---

14 Isaac Asimov, *Science and the Mountain Peak The Skeptical Inquirer*, Vol V No 2, W 80-1, p. 43.

15 For this account I am relying mostly on, Hugh Ross, *Genesis One, A Scientific Perspective* (Sierra Madre, Calif: Wisemen Productions, 1983) There are, however, other slightly different ways of viewing chapter one which also finds backing in science. For another version of Genesis 1 see, Peter Stoner, *Science Speaks, Scientific Proof of the Accuracy of Prophecy and the Bible* (Chicago: Moody Press, 1968) p. 11-53.

The wording of the Hebrew text indicates that God did not create these things out of nothing, as in verse 1. Instead, they were "formed" out of what God had already created. The actual process of their formation is not specified.

On the fourth day, we have the most criticized section of the account. The fourth day concerns the Sun and Moon. This is a problem. The account describes light as beginning on the second day and plant life on the third. Both of these occur before the Sun and the Moon on the fourth. How can there be plant life before the Sun?

One possible solution to this problem is to remember the perspective of the account: the planet's surface. As such, what we have on the fourth day is the appearance of the Sun, Moon, and stars in the sky (the breaking up of the cloud cover). As Gleason Archer has pointed out:

> Verse 16 should not be understood as indicating the creation of the heavenly bodies for the first time on the fourth creative day... The Hebrew verb *wayya'as* in v.16 should better be rendered "Now [God] *had made* the two great luminaries, etc." rather than as simple past tense, "[God] *made*."[16]

On the fifth day, God created animal life in the oceans, land, and air. During the first part of the sixth day, God created the more advanced animals, and near the end of the sixth day, God created human beings. Human beings are different from the earlier creations in that God created them in his image.

The sequence of events described in Genesis 1, including the sequence for the appearance of life, conforms well to the sequence of events described by scientists. While the description is too vague to be of any value to a scientist seeking knowledge of the Earth's early history, it gives a sketchy outline of that history.

The main points of the account are clear. Points such as God created the universe; He is responsible for the entire universe, including plants and animals. We are the final creation and different,

---

16   Gleason Archer, Encyclopedia of Bible Difficulties (Grand Rapids, MI: Regency, 1982) p. 61.

created in God's image. We are on solid ground as long as we stick to the text's main points.

On these points, there is considerable agreement within the Christian community. As you try to read more out of the text, the consensus begins to fade. Within the Christian community, most of the debate occurs around the length of the creation day.

A MATTER OF TIME

According to scientists, the Big Bang occurred about 14 billion years ago.[17] Does the Bible allow for such a great expanse of time? The answer depends on whom you ask. While traditionally, most Christians believed the creation day was 24 hours, this has not been a universally accepted position within the church.

Augustine, who lived and wrote in the fifth century A.D., and perhaps the most important theologian prior to Aquinas, apparently did not believe these days were the typical 24 hours days with which we are all familiar. Augustine wrote in his book, *The City of God*, concerning the length of the Genesis day,

> what kind of days these were it is extremely diffi-
> cult, or perhaps impossible for us to conceive, and how
> much more to say![18]

Still, while throughout the church's history, there have been those like Augustine questioning the literal 24-hour creation day, most Christians have accepted it. Why not?

After all, God could have created the world any way He wanted. If He had wanted to create the universe in six billion years, six million years, six years, six months, six days, six seconds, or even six microseconds, He could have. Until recently, scientists had very little to say on the matter; six literal 24-hour days was as good a choice as any.

Eventually, scientists became convinced that the world was much older than the few thousand years implied by a literal 24-

---

17   Brian Greene, The Fabric f the Cosmos (New York: Knoph, 2004) pp. 226
18   Augustine, *The City of God*, Book XI, Sections 6,7.

hour creation day. As scientists came to this conclusion, some Christians began to reexamine the other understanding suggested through the years. Today there are four main theories concerning the length of the day in Genesis 1.

One is, as just mentioned, the traditional view of a 24-hour day. This view is at odds with almost all of the scientific community. Still, a few scientists would accept an age of the Earth that is in the thousands of years instead of the billions.

A second theory is that while the creation days are still 24 hours long, the described creation is not the original. Supporters of this theory, sometimes referred to as the Gap Theory, believe that the original creation is described in Genesis 1:1, "In the beginning God created the heavens and the earth." This creation occurred over an unspecified period of time and at some unspecified time in the past.

Supporters of the Gap Theory believe that the original Earth lasted until a few thousand years ago. At that time, it was destroyed by some cosmic catastrophe rendering it, as is described in verse 2, "formless and empty." The period from creation until the destruction is not described in the Bible and represents a gap, thus the name Gap Theory, in the biblical record.

The Hebrew word in Genesis 1:2, usually translated *was*, can be translated as *became*. Consequently, if the Gap Theory is correct, the first two verses of Genesis should read:

> In the beginning God created the heavens and the
> earth. Now the earth *became* formless and empty.

The remainder of the chapter, rather than describing an original creation, describes a restoration process. Depending on how utter the destruction is or how complete the restoration is, one may or may not expect to find evidence of this process. Those who accept this theory have no problems with the theories of modern science concerning the age of the Earth.

The third theory also believes that the creation days were literal 24-hour days. In this view, the days do not represent the time during which God created; instead, they are the time during which God revealed the creation process to Moses.

According to the Revelational Day Theory, Moses received the knowledge of the creation through a series of revelations over six days. On each day, God revealed a different aspect of the creation. Since each day represents different aspects of creation, events are not necessarily described in the order of their occurrence but rather in their importance. Because of this, any differences in the order of creation between the Genesis account, and that proposed by science, would present no problem.

The last theory differs from the first three in that it rejects the belief that the creation days represent literal 24-hour days. This theory, often referred to as the Day-Age Theory, starts by pointing out that the Hebrew word for day used in Genesis 1, *yom,* does not always mean a 24-hour period. While *yom* can mean a 24-hour day, just like our own word, it can also mean a general period. Examples are phrases like "the day of the Lord," "this day and age," "In Washington's day," or "in my day."

The proponents of the Day-Age Theory have several reasons for believing that Moses was not using *yom* to mean 24 hours. Moses carefully follows the same literary formula for ending days one through six. "*And there was evening, and there was morning, the ___ day*" (Genesis 1:5, 8, 13, 19, 23, and 31).

Yet there is no ending at all for day seven. The seventh day was a day of rest. The writer of Hebrews speaks of this day of rest as lasting at least until his time (Hebrews 4:1-11). This has led the proponents of the Day-Age Theory to argue that the seventh day, or age, is still in progress and, therefore, the creation days must be longer than 24 hours.

Another reason for believing that Moses did not mean 24 hours is in the second chapter. There Moses begins a more detailed description of the creation of Adam and Eve. Moses starts by first summarizing the creation account,

> This is the account of the heavens and the earth
> when they were created, in the day that the LORD God

made earth and heaven. (Genesis 2:4 New American
Standard Version)

Here Moses collapses the entire creation process into a single
"day," indicating that he was not using the word to mean a single
24-hour period.

When one considers the events Moses describes taking place
between the creation of Adam and the creation of Eve, such as the
naming of the animals, it is hard to conceive of these events occurring in a single 24-hour period. Yet we are told that God created
both Adam and Eve on the sixth day. So again, it would seem that
Moses did not intend the word *yom* to mean 24 hours.

If Moses did not mean a 24-hour day, what did he mean?
Supporters of the Day-Age Theory believe that Moses only referred
to general periods or ages and that these ages could have been
extremely long. An age for the universe of billions of years would
present no problem at all.

Thus, there are four contending theories put forth by Christians to explain what was meant by Moses in his use of the word
yom. Of these four, only one, the literal 24-hour creation day,
conflicts with science concerning the age of the Earth.

These four theories are grounded in the assumption that
the creation account is a brief but scientific description of what
happened. Other Christians reject this. For some Christians, this
rejection is equivalent to rejecting a literal reading of the Bible.
Yet, as we said before, we should read and understand the Bible as
the authors intended, and most of the time, that is literally. But
is it here?

What did Moses intend when he wrote? Is it reasonable to
conclude that Moses intended this as a scientific description 3000
years before the scientific revolution? Concerning the main points
of the passage, the fact that God created everything and we are a
unique creation, created in God's image, is clear. Trying to force
that into a scientific mindset that did not exist at the time Moses
wrote is, at the very least anachronistic.

In this light, claiming Moses was scientifically wrong makes as much sense as saying Jesus was wrong because his parables were inaccurate depictions of historical events. Jesus did not intend them to be, nor was this their function.

Thus we have seen several ways of viewing the creation accounts that do not conflict with a universe billions of years old. As such, it is impossible to say the modern scientific view of an old Earth shows an error in the Bible.

EVOLUTION

By far, the most significant contention between Christians and modern science is the theory of evolution. Darwin's introduction of this theory in 1859 significantly affected the relationship between science and the Bible.

Skeptics immediately used evolution to attack Christianity directly. Indirectly, evolution formed the basis for many theories critical of religion we saw in earlier chapters. Today, many people view evolution as the central conflict between science and Christianity.

Any discussion of evolution is tricky because, on both sides, it is not always entirely clear what evolution means. When Carl Sagan states that "evolution is a fact, not a theory,"[19] it may sound definitive, but what does he mean by evolution? Is the belief that all dogs, whether poodles or great Danes, came from an original pair of dogs an evolutionary belief? The answer depends on whom you ask. I have heard yes and no answers from supporters and opponents of evolution.

Most evolution opponents would agree that all dogs came from some original dogs. In fact, as we will see shortly, some have no problem accepting that wolves and dogs came from a common source. This view would not be considered evolution per se but simply part of the normal variations that occur from generation to generation.

---

19 Carl Sagan, *Cosmos* (New York: Random House, 1980) p.27.

Where most opponents of evolution disagree with evolution-ists is the claim that one type of dog could evolve into something other than a dog. To go from a poodle to a collie is possible; to go from a dog to a cat is not. So, the disagreement is not over the con-cept of change in animals but over how much change is possible.

Supporters of evolution believe that the small or micro-changes occurring from generation to generation are additive and unlimit-ed. In other words, these changes will continue to occur so that, given enough generations, the many micro-changes will add up to large or macro-changes. In the end, you could have a vastly different type of animal.

One way to picture these different views of evolution is by comparing them to a game of dominos, where each domino is a new generation. For Darwin's view of evolution, we start with a single domino on an infinitely large floor. This domino represents some form of life. We then begin placing additional dominos on the floor, with each new domino representing some change.

Depending on where it is placed, each new domino might take us away from the original or move us closer. The farther we move away, the more change we have. If we move far enough away from the original, we will have so much change that we now have a new form of life.

Those rejecting evolution believe that micro-changes are not additive. As a result, macro-changes, changes that would result in a different kind of animal, cannot occur, at least not by the mech-anisms suggested by evolutionists.

If we return to our domino analogy, the change mechanism remains the same. Now, however, instead of playing on an infinite-ly large floor with plenty of room for new dominos or change, the game takes place on a table. While small changes still occur, they are limited by the size of the table. As a result, there will never be enough change to produce a new type of animal.

Opponents of evolution point to how with selective breeding, the more change you get, the more problems appear. These prob-lems limit the amount of change that is possible.

Since there is no dispute over the micro-changes that occur from generation to generation, we will define evolution in terms of macro-changes for this discussion. These changes result in one type of animal becoming another.

This definition still does not entirely resolve the problem. The concept of evolution has existed since ancient times. The claim that life started in simple forms, followed by complex forms, then still more complex forms, and finally, human beings is not controversial.

The Bible has life appearing in just this sort of "evolutionary" sequence. What Darwin did in 1859 was not to propose the concept of evolution as much as to propose a mechanism by which it could take place. He proposed evolution by natural selection.

Without a mechanism, evolution would simply be an interesting idea explaining very little. Add the concept of natural selection, and you have a meaningful theory and the source of the controversy. When I refer to evolution, I mean *a process through which macro-changes occur in life forms by the means of natural selection.*

When it comes to evolution and the Bible, two main questions arise. The first and foremost is: does the Bible conflict with the theory of evolution? Actually, the answer to this question is surprisingly straightforward: no.

If you are talking simply about a process by which life forms came to exist, nowhere does the Bible directly preclude the process of evolution. Evolution is simply not mentioned. The closest the Bible comes to denying evolution are the statements in Genesis that plants and animals were created "each according to kinds" (Genesis 1:11, 12, 21, 24, 25).

Yet precisely what is meant by the term "kind" in a scientific context? That is not clear. From a Christian point of view, God could have created the world any way He wanted to. The Bible clearly states that God created life; it does not say how.

The second question is: If Christianity philosophically has no problem with evolution, why do so many Christians, including this author, question evolution? Why is there a conflict at all? These are complex questions.

One reason is that both supporters and critics view evolution as much more than just a process by which life forms came into existence. Often they see evolution as a philosophical or even religious framework that excludes God from any influence in the origin of life. Naturally, Christians would reject any view of evolution that excluded God's influence since it conflicts with the Bible.

Another factor in Christian's rejection comes from how skeptics initially used the theory to attack Christianity. Thomas Huxley, also known as Darwin's Bulldog for his vigorous defense of evolution, when he first read the proof copies of Darwin's *Origin of Species*,

> was electrified by the book which bore on his own work. But even more than his direct professional interest, he was enamored by the book because he felt that it proved that the Bible was not literally correct and that species had evolved from earlier species instead of being specifically created.[20]

Both Christians and Atheists view evolution as playing a central role in the world views of secularism and atheism. As a result, the discussion often gets conflated with these other issues.

A third, and perhaps the most important, reason Christians reject evolution is its vulnerability to criticism, a vulnerability that has only gotten worse, not better, over time. Carl Sagan's statement that evolution is a fact is either not about evolution in the way we have defined it, or it is simply wrong.

When Darwin proposed his theory of evolution by natural selection, he realized that there was still a lot of work to be done. While the concept may have seemed reasonable, it remained to be proven. Since then, scientists have sought evidence that Darwin was right. But the evidence has not materialized. In fact, the evidence goes a long way toward showing that Darwin was wrong.

---

20 John Koster, *The Atheist Syndrome* (Brentwood, Tenn: Wolgemuth & Hyatt, 1989) p. 71.

Space does not permit us to go into all the problems faced by the theory of evolution, but we will summarize two of the main issues. The first is a classical argument against evolution, and the second is from recent scientific investigations.

HIDE AND SEEK

Perhaps the oldest argument against evolution is that it lacks physical support in the fossil record. In other words, scientists have found no transitional forms, sometimes referred to as missing links.

According to Darwin's theory, mutation and change occur in every generation. The natural struggle for survival would choose which of these changes improved the chances of staying alive. Life forms should be in a slow but constant state of flux.

These evolutionary changes are much too slow to be observed in action, for they take many generations to appear. Still, these changes should show up in the fossil record, where it is possible to compare species over long periods.

When Darwin proposed his theory, the fossil record was still relatively sparse. Supporters wrote off the absence of transitional forms as a lack of data. They believed that as they found more and more fossils, the transitional forms would become apparent.

This confirmation has not happened. As the search for fossils has proceeded over the 165 years since Darwin first published his theory, the gaps in the fossil record have become more pronounced. New species appear in the fossil record thoroughly developed and remain virtually unchanged for hundreds of millions of years until they suddenly disappear.

The fossil record simply does not show the slow, gradual changes with many transitional forms as predicted by Darwin. As biologist Michael Denton stated,

> The virtual complete absence of intermediate and ancestral forms from the fossil record is today recognized widely by many leading paleontologists as one of its most striking characteristics, so much so that those authorities who have adopted the cladistic framework now take it as axiomatic, that in attempting to deter-

mine the relationships of fossil species, in the words of
a recent British Museum publication: "we assume that
none of the fossil species we are considering is the an-
cestor of the other."[21]

Rather than a slow, gradual change, the fossil record shows
prolonged periods of stability marked by short periods of change.
The fossil record has led some paleontologists, particularly Niles
Eldredge and Stephen Jay Gould, to develop a new view of evolution. This new view, referred to as Punctuated Equilibrium, sees
evolution as occurring only for short periods (geologically speaking) with long periods of relative stability.

This new view is not so much a statement of evolution as it is
a description of the fossil record. It is more of a description because
it fails to explain why evolutionary changes occur only at certain
times or at all. The fossil record, rather than supporting the theory
of evolution, is strong evidence against it. The predicted transitional forms do not appear as the theory predicted they would.

BY THE NUMBERS

The second problem we will examine comes from recent developments in Molecular Biology. Advancements in this field now
permit molecular biologists to determine the precise amino acid
sequences making up a given protein. By comparing the different
protein sequences from different species, it is possible to determine
the relationships between different types of animals accurately.

Before these developments, the only way to determine these
relationships was through the somewhat subjective field of compar-
ative anatomy. Molecular Biology takes the guesswork out of the
process and makes it a matter of mathematical certainty.

The ability to determine the relationship between life forms to
a mathematical certainty had tremendous potential for the theory

---

21   Michael Denton, *Evolution, A Theory in Crisis* (Bethesda, Maryland:
     Adler & Adler, 1985) p. 165.

of evolution. Any evolutionary development should show up in these protein sequences.

Simple life forms should have protein sequences closer to each other than those in more advanced life forms like humans. Intermediate life forms should have sequences somewhere in the middle. The changes in these proteins would chart a clear progression from simple life, evolving into more intermediate forms, and finally into advanced life forms.

When scientists compare differences between the chemical makeup of the various proteins, they do not find a gradual divergence from simple to more advanced types of life. Instead, they find isolated groups at equal distances from each other. As biologist Michael Denton wrote concerning the variations of the protein cytochrome C,

> Again, an extraordinary mathematical exactness in the degree of isolation is apparent. So, although cytochrome C sequences varied among the different terrestrial vertebrates, all of them are equidistant from those of fish. At a molecular level there is no trace of the evolutionary transition from fish -> amphibian -> reptile -> mammal. So amphibia, always traditionally considered intermediate between fish and the other terrestrial vertebrates, are in molecular terms as far from fish as any group of reptiles or mammals! To those well acquainted with the traditional picture of vertebrate evolution the result is truly astonishing.[22]

Once again, the scientific evidence does not support an evolutionary view of the world and argues against it. And the problems for evolution continue to grow.

Michael Behe's work on the irreducible complexity of particular biological systems, discussed in the last chapter,[23] and Jonathan Wells' book, *Icons of Evolution*, are recent examples. Wells' book exposes the exaggerations, errors, and in some cases, outright fraud

---

22 Michael Denton, *Evolution, A Theory in Crisis* (Bethesda, Maryland: Adler & Adler, 1985) p. 285.

23 Michael Behe, *Darwin's Black Box: The Biochemical Challenge to Evolution* (New York: The Free Press, 1996).

behind some well-known evidence used to support evolution commonly found in textbooks.[24]

Neither of these men are theologians but scientists trained in the fields in which they write. Behe is an associate professor of Biochemistry, while Wells is a biologist with PhDs from Yale and the University of California at Berkeley.

In addition, it is important to note that it is not just Christians who question the theory of evolution. Scientific knowledge today is so vast that no one can keep fully abreast of the work done outside their field of specialization. This specialization has led to an interesting development noted by Professor Charles Thaxton,

> many scientists are expert in their own areas and quite ignorant of what is happening in neighboring disciplines. This is not a pejorative statement about scientists but a comment on how rapidly knowledge is accumulating. What we find, as a result is a tendency for scientists to accept the traditional evolutionary view in most areas, *but* (and this is significant!) often questioning this scientific orthodoxy in their own area of expertise.[25]

Michael Denton, who I have quoted in this chapter, does not argue that evolution is false from a Christian or religious position. He does not make any religious arguments at all and is an agnostic. Denton's position is that we do not know enough to determine how we came to be here. According to Denton,

> The truth is that despite the prestige of evolutionary theory and the tremendous intellectual effort directed towards reducing living systems to the confines of Darwinian thought, nature refuses to be imprisoned. In the final analysis we still know very little about how new forms of life arise. The "mystery of mysteries" – the origin of new beings on earth – is still largely as enigmatic as when Darwin set sail on the Beagle.[26]

---

24   Jonathan Wells, *Icons of Evolution, Science or Myth? Why much of what we teach about evolution is wrong* (Washington D.C.: Regnery Publishing, 2000).

25   Charles Thaxton, in *The Intellectuals Speak Out About God* ed. Roy Abraham Varghese (Dallas, Texas: Lewis and Stanley, 1984) p. 5.

26   Michael Denton, *Evolution, A Theory in Crisis* (Bethesda, Maryland: Adler & Adler, 1985) pp. 358-9.

The main reason Christians reject the theory of evolution is its lack of support in scientific or biblical evidence. Of course, if you can only accept a natural explanation, you have only two choices. Accept evolution, or like Denton, wait for more information.

Since the second edition's publication, these problems have only grown, particularly in microbiology. The ability to sequence DNA permitted a much better understanding of the changes seen in various animals.

For example, scientists have sequenced the DNA of various types of bears. From the perspective of evolution, the question becomes, for example: How did the various colors of different bears evolve? How did the polar bear (*Ursus maritimus*) adapt to the arctic region and become white, while the brown bear is brown?

They have found the cause of the variation of color from one type of bear to the next. Surprisingly it comes from the corruption of gene sequences. Earlier generations of bears possessed gene sequences, which became degraded in various ways over the generations. These changes are degradations because the original gene can no longer perform its function.

Thus take the gene that determines the color of the fur. Degrade it, and it can no longer perform that function. The bear ends up white. The degradations in the various genes result in different characteristics we now see in bears. As Behe summed up the matter,

> It seems, then, that the magnificent *Ursus maritimus* has adjusted to its harsh environment mainly by degrading genes that its ancestors already possessed. Despite its impressive abilities, rather than *evolving*, it has adapted predominately by *devolving*.[27]

These changes are a form of evolution; thus, this discovery supports a limited view of evolution. However, it only supports micro-evolution. It shows how one type of bear can evolve into all the various types we see worldwide. Thus, it supports a form of evolution over which there is little, if any, controversy.

---

27 Michael J. Behe, *Darwin Devolves,* (New York, HaperOne, 2019) p. 17.

It does not support macro-evolution, the origin of new life forms. In this case, while this discovery explains the origin of all the types of bears, it does not explain how the bear came to exist in the first place. From a genetic perspective, the various bears came about due to the degradation of various genes. But how did the various genes come to be there first?

Scientists classify life into a hierarchy with Domain at the highest level. Below this is Kingdom, Phylum, Class, Order, Family, Genus, and the lowest being Species. The degradation of genes to produce variations in life, such as the various types of dogs or bears, seems limited to the family level and below.

> What variation can exist within a family? For the dog family, it's the difference between a domestic dog and a wolf and a fox. For the cat family, it's the difference between a lion and a leopard and a lynx. For the seal family, it's the difference between a ringed seal and a hooded seal and a bearded seal. That degree of variation can likely be achieved by random mutation and natural selection.[28]

So, the degradation of genes can explain how we got wolves and sheepdogs. Still, it does not explain how the base genetic material got there in the first place. It does not explain the origins of the genes that degraded to produce the various types of animals in the dog family.

This variation produced by degradation was the basis for Darwin's theory. But it cannot be a complete explanation. Saying degradation is an explanation for all of life is like saying a car driving on a flat tire explains the origin of the car. The process of breaking cannot explain the process of creation.

Again, we have only briefly examined a couple of problems. Given such problems, is it any wonder that some Christians feel no compulsion to fall in line and accept such a tenuous theory?

---

28   Behe, Michael J. *Darwin Devolves (The New Science About DNA That Challenges Evolution)* HarperCollins. Kindle Edition. p. 156.

CONCLUSION

The relationship between science and the Bible is complex and is the subject of much discussion within the Christian community. Often Christians are stereotyped as a closed-minded, unified mass who demand conformity and cannot tolerate differing opinions. While it is true that there are some Christians like this, they are not the norm.

Supporters of the different theories concerning the age of the Earth may disagree with each other on their understanding of the creation account in Genesis, but this does not prevent them from worshiping together. It is not uncommon to find people representing two or more of these theories worshiping in any given church. For most Christians, these issues are just not that important.

On a purely intellectual basis, one could ask: Who is closed-minded? From a Christian point of view, there is no problem accepting an age of the Earth that is either young or old. God could have created it either way, and Christians are on both sides of this issue.

A secular scientist must accept an old Earth, for they cannot conceive how physical processes could have created the Earth any faster. A Christian can accept an origin of life by natural or supernatural processes. Again, God could have done it either way. Even though the evidence is currently against it, secular scientists can only consider natural processes.

These questions are matters of open debate where Christians can and do take differing positions. For the scientific community, for the most part, the debate on these issues is restricted to a narrow and limited area, and only certain positions are "acceptable."

Can a group discussing an issue from multiple sides legitimately be labeled closed-minded by a group for whom the issue is settled with little or no room for debate?

Strangely, Christians are frequently labeled as closed-minded and intolerant for simply questioning evolution. If evolution is firmly established, why must its adherents fight so hard to keep contrary views from being heard?

The Bible is concerned mainly with communicating knowledge of God. It simply does not concern itself with attempting to convey scientific information. This is not to say that the Bible makes scientific errors, but only that it does not address scientific questions directly. As for the contention that modern scientific advances have disproven the Bible, this is not the case. If anything, the opposite is true.

It has not been possible in the limited space here to cover all of the alleged problems between science and the Bible. Still, I think we have seen that accepting the Bible as God's Word does not force you to abandon the findings of modern science. Many Christians see no fundamental problems between science and the Bible. While other Christians do see problems with some of the findings of science, this diversity of opinion is not an excuse to reject the Bible.

If anything, it only strengthens the contention that the Bible does not speak clearly on scientific issues. As we have said, this was not the Bible's purpose. When the Bible speaks about our relationship with God, it is very clear and can be relied upon. Modern science has found nothing to disprove this.

6

IS THE BIBLE RELIABLE?

*History is the witness that testifies to the passing
of time; it illumines reality, vitalizes memory, provides
guidance in daily life, and brings in tidings of antiquity.
(Marcus Tullius Cicero 106-43 B.C.)*

WHILE MOST PEOPLE PROBABLY KNOW who Julius
Caesar was, the first Caesar, and are somewhat familiar
with Nero, the last of the original ruling family, few know
the names of those who ruled between them. Yet, while few know
the names of the rulers of the Roman Empire during the first half
of the first century A.D., most people probably know the name
of the Roman governor who ruled a small region at the edge of
the empire called Judea from A.D. 26 to A.D. 36. His name was
Pontius Pilate.

Appointed by Tiberius Caesar, Pilate was the fifth Roman governor to rule Judea. This region had fallen to Rome in 63 B.C.,
defeated by an army led by the Roman general Pompey. While
the area was under the control of Rome, it never seemed to benefit
from the Pax Romana – The Peace of Rome.

The area was in constant turmoil. Finally, to bring peace,
Rome put Herod the Great in charge. Herod ruled from 37 B.C.
to 4 B.C. After his death, Herod's kingdom was divided among
his sons. The son who ruled the area around Jerusalem soon made
such a mess of things that a Roman governor replaced him.

Several ancient historians mention Pilate. The Roman historian Tacitus wrote that the Romans crucified Christ during the rule
of Pontius Pilate.[1] The Jewish historian Josephus mentions Pilate in

---

1   Tacitus, *Annals*, 15.44.

two books, *The Wars of the Jews* and *Antiquities of the Jews*.[2] Josephus records Pilate's arrival, departure, and some of the events of his rule, including the crucifixion of Jesus.[3]

Despite all of this, some have questioned the historical existence of Pilate.[4] During the last century and early part of this century, radical critics questioned everything in the Bible. Some even claimed that there never was a person named Jesus.

These critics claimed that there is no evidence that Jesus ever existed and that the writers of the New Testament made him up. All references to Jesus outside the Bible came from the New Testament accounts.

Since the references to Pilate commonly occurred along with references to Jesus, which they believed were historically unreliable, they concluded that the references to Pilate must also be unreliable. They concluded that Pilate never existed.

In 1961, Italian archaeologists excavating the coastal city of Caesarea settled the question of the historical existence of Pilate once and for all. During the dig, they unearthed a stone whose left side was severely damaged, so the left side was no longer readable. The right half contained the following words:

> ...S TIBERIEVM
> ...TIVS PILATVS
> ...ECTVS IVDA...E[5]

While badly damaged, the top line contains the letter S followed by the name of the Roman emperor Tiberius (TIBERIEVM). The middle line contains the name of Pontius Pilate (*pon*TIVS PI-

---

2   Josephus, *The Wars of the Jews* 2.9.2-4 and *The Antiquities of the Jews* 18.3.1-3.

3   The passage concerning the crucifixion of Jesus has been questioned. For a complete discussion of this passage see Christianity and Secularism, Consider Christianity Series, Volume 2.

4   John Warwick Montgomery, *The Jury Returns: A Juridical Defense of Christianity in Evidence for Faith*, edited by John Warwick Montgomery (Dallas, Texas: Probe, 1991) p. 326.

5   J. A. Thompson, *The Bible and Archaeology*, 3rd ed. (Grand Rapids, MI: Eerdmans, 1982) p. 311.

LATVS). The final line once read *praef*ECTVS IVDA*ea*E, Pilate's official title as governor. There is no doubt that the Gospels are accurate in their references to a Roman governor named Pilate.

With discoveries like the Pilate stone, archaeology has dramatically increased our understanding of and confidence in the Bible. But archaeology cannot be expected to confirm individual events.

The passage of time destroyed most of the evidence. As we just saw, only half of the Pilate stone has survived. What if we lost the entire stone? As such, we cannot depend on archaeology alone.

So how can we determine if the New Testament documents are reliable? This question affects more than the Bible; any time we consider an ancient text, we must assess its accuracy. So how is this done?

The first step in this process is to determine the type of writing. A historian considering the following three works, *Aesop's Fables,* Julius Caesar's *Gallic Wars,* and Tacitus' *Annals,* would consider Tacitus the most reliable.

Fables are stories that contain no historical content. Fables differ from myths in that fables are fictional stories, usually teaching some truth, such as the importance of being prepared. Myths are stories meant to explain things. Technically, a true story could still be a myth, as the definition centers around the explanation, not the historicity.

Caesar's *Gallic Wars* is an autobiographical account of his conquest of Gaul, while Tacitus' *Annals* are historical writings. While both Caesar and Tacitus are writing about historical events, Caesar is writing about himself and is consequently more likely to distort the events to favor himself.

When we come to the Bible, determining the type of writing is not as simple. This difficulty is because the Bible contains a wide variety of writings. Some books like Exodus and Kings contain history, Psalms is poetry, and many New Testament 'books' are letters.

Many books contain a mixture of different styles. The Gospels not only contain the accounts of the life and teachings of Jesus Christ, but they also have some of the parables that Jesus taught.

Parables are not intended to be historical; they teach some truth, usually moral.

As a result, there is no clear consensus on the writing in the Bible, and many believe it is its own type.[6] While scholars can generally determine the literary type for individual passages, some are unclear. For example, Luke 16:19-31 contains the account of the Rich Man and Lazarus. While many translations label this a parable, some scholars are unsure.

One thing is clear; many biblical writers wrote about historical events. Both the Hebrew Scripture and the New Testament are based on fundamental events that are seen as historical. In the Hebrew Scriptures and Judaism, the defining event was the Exodus. In the New Testament and Christianity, it is the resurrection of Jesus. The writers of both testaments considered these events to be historical.

The New Testament writers not only considered the resurrection to be historical, but they also considered it verifiable. The Apostle Paul, in his first letter to the church in Corinth, wrote about the resurrection.

Contrary to some, he was not writing to those who already agreed but addressing those who didn't. Because of the prevalence of Greek thought that downplayed the physical, some in Corinth believed the resurrection of a physical body was not an essential belief.

In his letter, Paul included a defense of the Resurrection, pointing out that Jesus appeared to over 500 people, many of whom were still alive (1Cor 15:3-6). The clear implication was that if anyone had trouble believing the resurrection, as some of the Corinthians did, they could test what Paul said by going and talking to the hundreds of people who saw it.

Clearly, the biblical authors intended much of what they wrote to be considered historical. We should approach their writings as we would any other ancient work that claims to record history.

---

6   Craig Blomberg, *The Historical Reliability of the Gospels* (Downers Grove, Illinois: Inter-Varsity, 1987) p. 239

While this conclusion seems simple, it is more important than it may initially seem.

It is important because scholars generally consider ancient historical accounts accurate unless there are reasons to believe otherwise. The burden of proof rests with those who believe them inaccurate.

Not only is this a legitimate assumption, but it is also a necessary one. We do not have enough ancient records to document everything thoroughly. Much of what we know concerning ancient times we know from only a single source.

We cannot take this *burden of proof* concept too rigidly. It does not mean we accept everything unless there is absolute proof that it is wrong. This concept is just a starting point for the examination.

Perhaps a better way to look at this is in terms of *the benefit of the doubt*. If, after examining an account of an ancient writer, there are reasons to believe the writer is reliable, and we can find no good reason to reject it, then the benefit of the doubt should go to the writer.

INERRANCY VS. RELIABILITY

An additional issue is the concept of Inerrancy. Many believers and critics alike believe that if even the smallest error is anywhere in the Bible, it cannot be the word of God or be trusted. That is not what we are arguing for here.

To be clear, I believe in the inerrancy of the Bible, at least when it is carefully defined, such as in the *Chicago Statement on Biblical Inerrancy*.[7] The statement resulted from a conference of 200 evangelical leaders in 1978 and is eleven pages long, consisting of 29 articles. As one can see from its length, the concept of Inerrancy is not as simple as the Bible does not make errors.

Given the large variety of subjects, styles, and types of writings in the Bible, the timespan over which the authors wrote, and

---

7   The Chicago Statement on Biblical Inerrancy, https://library.dts.edu/
     Pages/TL/Special/ICBI_1.pdf.

the changing social conditions of the audiences, we must consider many factors.

These factors are a significant reason the term is negative: inerrancy, meaning without error. We cannot just claim biblical statements are always true because the Bible sometimes records the lies that people told, as we will see shortly. Thus Inerrancy holds that the Bible faithfully recorded these lies, not that the lies are true.

There is also the whole issue of what is truth, a vast and complex subject. The third book in this series, *Faith and Reason,* touches on this subject, and another book *Seeking Truth*, deals with it in much greater detail.

Then there is the distinction between what the original author, inspired by God, intended to say and what I understand 2000 years later when reading the Bible. Even if the Bible is inerrant, our understanding of it is not. This distinction is clear from the many disagreements believers have concerning the meaning of some passages.

One of these disagreements concerns the meaning of inspiration itself, about which many different views exist. These views range from concepts close to that of an artist inspired by a landscape to those closer to dictation.

The former view would allow for errors, seeing them due to the writer, but the message inspired by God is correct. Then some Christians believe that God is learning like the rest of us and thus can make mistakes.

In short, while Christians believe the Bible is inspired, not all Christians accept that inspiration mean the Bible is inerrant.

. Some think there are errors in the Bible. In contrast, others allow for the theoretical possibility, even if they don't know of any. The bottom line is that there are many views on inspiration and inerrancy .

To accept inerrancy requires accepting certain beliefs about God and depends on a particular understanding of passages in the Bible. Demanding non-believers accept these as a condition for salvation is intellectually backward, effectively getting the cart before the horse.

Because of such factors, while I accept inerrancy, I do not argue for inerrancy with non-Christians. Instead, I argue reliability is all that is needed.

Suppose the Bible is reliable in its statements concerning Jesus, his life, death, resurrection, and the message of salvation. If one accepts these, is their salvation threatened because they think a writer may have made an insignificant error in some account? As we shall see, the Bible is very reliable.

DETERMINING RELIABILITY

There are many ways to judge the accuracy of an ancient historical record. Scholars generally grouped these into three areas: bibliographical, external, and internal. Bibliographical questions concern the reliability of the text. Does the text we have accurately reflect what the author originally wrote? As we saw in the first chapter, the answer here is yes.

External tests involve comparing the account in question to other accounts of ancient history and the findings of archaeology. Where possible, archaeology has shown the biblical accounts quite reliable. The only real problem with external tests is that often there are no external sources to compare. As a result, no confirmation is possible.

That leaves the internal tests. While scholars can apply many internal tests to a document, the first and most crucial test is internal consistency. Does a document present a single consistent account of events, or does it contradict itself?

The reliability of the Bible is often questioned by those claiming that the different authors contradict each other and sometimes even contradict themselves. In other words, the authors of the Bible could not get the story straight. This argument is one of the most pervasive myths concerning the Bible.

ALLEGED CONTRADICTIONS

This belief is hard to disprove because most people cannot cite a single example of a contradiction. They just know they exist.

Whenever anyone tells me that the Bible contains contradictions, I ask for an example. Only a few people have been able to cite one, and we will examine some of these alleged contradictions shortly. Most people are amazed that anyone would even attempt to maintain that the Bible does not contradict itself.

Another reason this belief is so hard to dispel is that even after reconciling a supposed contradiction, often the attitude is there must be many more.

It is not as if any of these supposed contradictions are new, as they have been around for hundreds of years, and scholars answered them long ago.

Before we go any further, we should make clear what is and is not a contradiction.[8] A contradiction exists when two or more statements differ, so they cannot all be correct. The statements *"An earthquake destroyed San Francisco in 1906"* and *"There was no earthquake in San Francisco in 1906"* contradict each other because both cannot be correct.

Still, not all statements that differ are contradictions. The statements *"An earthquake destroyed San Francisco in 1906"* and *"A fire destroyed San Francisco in 1906"* differ in their descriptions of what destroyed San Francisco in 1906. These statements do not constitute a contradiction, for both could be correct.

As it turns out, both of these statements are correct. One of the results of the 1906 earthquake in San Francisco was a devastating fire that destroyed a large part of the city. Rather than being a contradiction, these statements are complimentary. Separately they

---

8   What most people mean when they use the term contradiction is, in a strict logical sense, a contrary. A contradiction exists between two statements when one statement must be true and the other false. Two statements are contrary if they both cannot be true. In a contrary both statements can be false. For clarity, we will use the term contradiction as it is popularly understood to include both contradictions and contrary.

each provide part of the entire story. Taken together, they give us a more complete picture of the separately described event.

While this distinction between a difference and a contradiction may seem obvious, it is nevertheless overlooked by many who claim that the accounts in the Bible are contradictory.

For example, in his book *The Case Against Christianity*, Michael Martin cites a supposed contradiction between Matthew and Luke as a reason to reject the Virgin Birth of Jesus. According to Martin,

> in Matthew, the news of the coming birth of Jesus is conveyed to Joseph in a dream; in Luke, Mary is told directly by the Angel Gabriel.[9]

While it is true that these two accounts are different, where is the contradiction? How does Joseph's dream about the birth preclude Mary from being told by an angel? Luke records,

> In the sixth month of Elizabeth's pregnancy, God sent the angel Gabriel to Nazareth, a town in Galilee, to a virgin pledged to be married to a man named Joseph, a descendant of David. The virgin's name was Mary. The angel went to her and said, "Greetings, you who are highly favored! The Lord is with you."

The angel then proceeds to tell Mary she will give birth to Jesus. The account in Matthew begins with the following,

> This is how the birth of Jesus Christ came about: His mother Mary was found to be with child through the Holy Spirit. Because Joseph her husband was a righteous man and did not want to expose her to public disgrace, he had in mind to divorce her quietly. But after he had considered this, an angel of the Lord appeared to him in a dream. (Matthew 1:18-20)

Again, the accounts are different, but where is the contradiction? It would appear that an angel visited Mary and told her about the virgin birth, as recorded in Luke. When she told Joseph about this, not too surprisingly, he had trouble with the idea that his wife-to-be was "with child of the Holy Spirit." As a result, an

---

9   Michael Martin, *The Case Against Christianity* (Philadelphia, Temple University Press, 1991) p. 107.

angel visited Joseph in a dream to calm his fears. There is no contradiction here. Martin acknowledges,

> It is perhaps possible to reconcile the two accounts
> of the announcement of the Virgin Birth by saying that
> Mary and Joseph were notified in different ways. How-
> ever, there is certainly no suggestion of this in the two
> Gospels; they lead one to believe that *only* one notifi-
> cation was made. Indeed, it seems likely that if there
> were two independent notifications of the Virgin Birth,
> this would have been mentioned in at least one of the
> two Gospels. (Emphasis in original)[10]

Where is the indication that there was only one notification?
Why must a writer mention both accounts? Martin's claim depends
on a lot of assumptions, and questionable ones at that.

Matthew's perspective is Jesus' royal lineage, traced through
Joseph. Therefore, he mentions Joseph's notification. Why would
he need to mention Mary's notification?

Luke mentions that other accounts already existed. Some
scholars believe that one of these was Matthew. Whether Matthew or not, these other accounts may have mentioned Joseph's
notification. In any event, he was focusing more on Mary.

All writers face the decision of what to include and what to
leave out. That a particular writer did not include all the details a
modern critic thinks they should, does not make them wrong or
mean there is a contradiction. Yet, such thinking is the basis for
many such claims.

During the nineteenth century, rationalism was at its height,
and attacking the Bible was a popular pastime among many intellectuals. In 1859, William Henry Burr, a newspaper reporter and
critic of the Bible, anonymously published, *Self-Contradictions of
the Bible.* In this pamphlet, Burr listed 144 places where he believed the Bible contradicted itself.

His style was simple and straightforward. He just listed the
passages he believed contradicted each other, preceding each passage with a short headline to highlight the contradiction. For a

---

10   Michael Martin, *The Case Against Christianity* (Philadelphia, Temple
     University Press, 1991) p. 107-8.

well-known alleged contradiction that we will examine shortly, Burr stated:

> PAUL'S ATTENDANTS HEARD THE MIRACULOUS
> VOICE, AND STOOD SPEECHLESS.
> And the men which journeyed with him [Paul]
> stood speechless, hearing a voice but seeing no man.
> (Acts 9:7.)
> PAUL'S ATTENDANTS HEARD **NOT** THE VOICE,
> AND WERE PROSTRATE.
> And they that were with me saw indeed the light
> and were afraid; but they heard not the voice of him that
> spake to me. (Acts 22:9) And when we were all fallen to
> the earth, I heard a voice. (Acts 26:14)[11]

In response to Burr's pamphlet, and others like it circulating at the time, John W. Haley began to compile all of the alleged contradictions he could find. He then developed responses to them.

Initially published in 1874, Haley's *Alleged Discrepancies of the Bible*[12] remains the most complete work on the subject, listing hundreds of supposed contradictions and their answers.[13]

The vast majority of these contradictions take minimal effort to reconcile. In fact, only the most cursory of readings will lead to a contradiction. Reading the verses in context eliminates most contradictions entirely.

One of my college professors used a perfect example of this type of supposed contradiction to show the Bible was full of contradictions. The contradiction concerns the accounts of King Saul's death recorded in 1 Samuel and 2 Samuel. In 1 Samuel, King Saul was wounded during a battle, and the Philistines were going to capture him. Rather than be taken prisoner, Saul told his armor-bearer to kill him.

---

11 William Henry Burr, Self Contradictions of the Bible (Buffalo NY: Prometheus Books, 1987) p. 67.

12 John W Haley, *Alleged Discrepancies of the Bible* (Grand Rapids, MI: Baker Books, 1977).

13 While Haley's work is the most complete, it does not always give the best answer. One reason for this in the tremendous advances in biblical scholarship, languages, and archaeology that have been made since Haley's writing.

> But his armor-bearer was terrified and would not
> do it; so Saul took his own sword and fell on it. When
> the armor-bearer saw that Saul was dead, he too fell on
> his sword and died with him. (1 Samuel 31:4,5)

In the book of 2 Samuel, we find that after Saul was wounded, an Amalekite approached him. Saul called to the Amalekite,

> 'Stand over me and kill me! I am in the throes of
> death but I'm still alive.'
> "So I stood over him and killed him because I knew
> that after he had fallen he could not survive." (2 Samuel
> 1:9,10)

In 1 Samuel, Saul kills himself, while in 2 Samuel, we are told that an Amalekite killed Saul. One of these accounts is obviously wrong unless Saul dies twice, which is a contradiction.

Still, is this a contradiction that shows the Bible is unreliable? We must remember that the books we refer to as 1 & 2 Samuel were originally one book and that the same writer wrote both accounts. Is it likely that a writer would write two contradictory accounts, one right after the other, by mistake?

When we take a closer look at these two accounts, we find there is no real problem, at least with the writer's reliability. The account in 1 Samuel records the death of Saul as a suicide, and this is how Saul died.

In 2 Samuel, the author is not recording Saul's death, but instead, a report given to David by an Amalekite. From the account, it is evident that the Amalekite was lying. The author of Samuel records his lie faithfully.

Why would the Amalekite take credit for killing Saul, especially considering that David had him executed for the act? Many knew Saul had been trying to have David killed for years. With the death of Saul, David would now be king.

The Amalekite had evidently come upon King Saul's body shortly after he had committed suicide. After taking Saul's crown and armbands, he rushed off to David to take credit for eliminating David's worst enemy. Unfortunately for the Amalekite, he misread the situation. Although Saul wanted to kill David, David had no desire to kill Saul.

While the statement of the Amalekite does conflict with the account of Saul's death given by the author of Samuel, this does not lead to a conclusion that the Bible contradicts itself and cannot be trusted.

The author of Samuel does not make two contradictory claims concerning Saul's death. Instead, he tells us how Saul died and then records the claim made by an Amalekite that he had killed Saul.

This account points out that a contradiction can be read into the text if one ignores the context of the verses. This also reveals another problem when dealing with contradictions.

Many of these supposed contradictions are taught as fact by scholarly people. It is so "well known" that the Bible contains contradictions that few question the examples.

This is not a problem confined to lay people, for many biblical scholars also accept these alleged contradictions without question and without researching them. The Old Testament scholar Gleason Archer, in response to some alleged contradictions raised by two other scholars, wrote,

> None of these alleged problems have been un-noticed or unanswered by Bible scholars of former generations. Since, however, they have been raised anew in the current debate, it seems appropriate to deal with them once again.[14]

After dealing with several alleged contradictions in the Gospels, The New Testament scholar Craig Blomberg wrote concerning some of his fellow scholars,

> It is strange how often the reliability of the gospels is impugned by scholars who believe them to be hopelessly contradictory yet who have never seriously interacted with the types of solutions proposed here.[15]

14 Gleason L. Archer, *Alleged Errors and Discrepancies in the Original Manuscripts of the Bible* in *Inerrancy*, edited by Norman L. Geisler (Grand Rapids, MI: Academie, 1980) p. 60.

15 Craig Blomberg, *The Historical Reliability of the Gospels* (Downers Grove, Illinois: Inter-Varsity, 1987) p. 150.

These supposed contradictions become the basis for much of modern scholarship. The French historian Charles Guignebert is an excellent example of this in his book, *Jesus.*

During his discussion of the Christian testimony for Jesus, Guignebert ridicules the Catholic Church's support for Luke's authorship of the Book of Acts. As Guignebert writes,

> A decision of the *Papal Biblical Commission* of June 12th, 1913, states that the author of Acts is definitely Saint Luke the Evangelist, that the work cannot be attributed to more than one author, the contrary supposition having been found to be *wholly baseless*, and that its agreement with the Epistles of Paul is remarkable. It is less remarkable, however, than the audacity of such assertions, since it has been established that the author of Acts was ignorant of the Epistles of Paul, and even formally contradicts them.[16]

To support his claim that the author of Acts knew nothing about Paul's epistles and contradicted them, Guignebert refers the reader in a footnote to Acts 2:4 and 1 Corinthians 12:10 & 30. When we examine this supposed contradiction, again, we find that only a superficial reading, out of context, will produce a contradiction. Consider the verses,

> Acts 2:4   All of them were filled with the Holy Spirit and began to speak in other tongues as the Spirit enabled them.
>   1 Corinthians 12:10 ...to another miraculous powers, to another prophecy, to another distinguishing between spirits, to another speaking in different kinds of tongues, and to still another the interpretation of tongues.
>   1 Corinthians 12:30 Do all have the gifts of healing? Do all speak in tongues? Do all interpret?

Apparently, Guignebert believes that the Catholic Church, blinded by its faith, could not see that the author of Acts taught that everyone should speak in tongues. In contrast, Paul taught that only some people would.

---

16 Charles Guignebert, *Jesus* Trans. S Hooke (New Hyde Park, New York: University Books; 1956) p. 22.

Unfortunately, for Guignebert to conclude that these verses contradict one another, you must completely ignore the context and purpose for which these verses were written, along with the rules of logic.

In Acts, Luke describes a particular and extraordinary event: the day of Pentecost. In 1 Corinthians, Paul writes about the church's general rules governing behavior.

The general rule is that everyone does not receive the gift of tongues. This rule in no way precludes everyone at a particular event, like the day of Pentecost, could speak in tongues. To claim that these verses contradict each other is to commit the logical fallacy of composition: confusing the general with the specific.

Since his claim depends on a logical fallacy, it is irrational. Couldn't Guignebert have found a better example of a contradiction to prove that people who disagree with him are audacious?

Perhaps the most well-known alleged contradiction, or at least the one I have heard most often, concerns the conversion of the apostle Paul. In the Book of Acts, Luke tells us that the apostle Paul, known then as Saul, encountered the resurrected Christ on his way to Damascus to arrest Christians. This event resulted in his conversion. As for Paul's companions, the King James Version states:

> And the men which journeyed with him stood speechless, hearing a voice, but seeing no man (Acts 9:7 KJV)

Many years later, while on a trip to Jerusalem, some Jews falsely accused Paul of bringing Gentiles into the temple. While speaking to the crowd in his defense, Paul recalled his dramatic conversion saying, again in the King James Version,

> And they that were with me saw indeed the light, and were afraid; but they heard not the voice of him that spake to me. (Acts 22:9 KJV)

The first account describes Paul's companions as "*hearing a voice,*" while in the other, "*they heard not the voice.*" While at first, this seems like a clear contradiction, these two verses are really very easy to reconcile.

You may have noticed that I quoted both of these verses from the King James Version. This is because the contradiction does not appear in the original Greek, nor many modern translations. The New International Version, the version used in this book, renders the second quotation as:

> My companions saw the light, but they did not understand the voice of him who was speaking to me. (Acts 22:9 NIV)

What we have here is not a contradiction but a poor translation in the King James Version.

Like the English word *hear*, the Greek word *akouo* (ἀκούω), from which we get the word acoustic, takes on different meanings depending on how one uses it. In the first quotation, *akouo* is with the genitive case and means *to perceive sound*. In the second quotation, *akouo* is in the accusative case and means *to understand*.[17] Therefore, the men with Paul heard the voice but did not understand it. Many of these supposed contradictions have disappeared as we have learned more about the ancient Hebrew and Greek languages.

Many alleged contradictions result from the fact that the accounts given in the Bible are, for the most part, only summaries of the actual events. The writers of the Bible did not write from a purely historical point of view; they wrote with the intent to teach about God. When writing about an event, they did not see it necessary to include every little detail, but only those important to the writer's message.

As with the two accounts concerning the notification of Jesus' birth discussed above, this does not mean that the accounts are somehow in error. Anytime an event is written about, whether in a newspaper story or a history textbook, limited space, and the reader's patience, dictate that some details must be left out.

---

17   Gleason L. Archer, *Encyclopedia of Bible Difficulties* (Grand Rapids, MI: Regency, 1982) p. 382

Many newspaper stories concerning the assassination of President Kennedy included the fact that Governor Connally of Texas was also shot. Yet many history books, when they discuss the assassination of Kennedy, don't even bother to mention that Connally was present. No one would claim that these accounts contradict each other or that they are wrong.

For the Bible, critics label such a difference a contradiction and proof you cannot trust what it says. A typical example of this type of supposed contradiction can be seen in the accounts of Jesus healing the blind man as he left the city of Jericho. As described by Burr:

> TWO BLIND MEN BESOUGHT JESUS
> And behold, *two blind men* sitting by the wayside, when they heard that Jesus passed by, cried out, saying, Have mercy on us, O Lord thou son of David. (Matthew 20:30)
> ONLY **ONE** BLIND MAN BESOUGHT HIM
> A certain blind man sat by the wayside begging... And he cried out, Jesus, thou son of David, have mercy on me. (Luke 18: 35,38)[18]

Rather than being a contradiction, this is a case where one author presents more information than another. In this case, Matthew gives us a more complete account mentioning both blind men, while Luke mentions only one. It is important to note that Luke does not say, as is claimed by Burr, that only one blind man called to Jesus.

This type of alleged contradiction is probably the most common. It is raised whenever one author leaves out or simplifies something another author mentions. For example, many critics see a contradiction when Matthew mentions that Joseph and Mary fled with Jesus into Egypt while Luke skips over this period. Since the writers of the Bible had to be selective, it should not be surprising that they did not all write about the same events or include the same details.

To a large extent, this is a no-win situation. Until his death in 1989, Dr. Walter Martin was one of Christianity's leading defend-

---

18   William Henry Burr, *Self Contradictions of the Bible* (Buffalo NY: Prometheus Books, 1987) p. 60.

ers. He often pointed out that if two biblical authors agree, some critics will claim that one must have copied from the other and will call both into question. Yet, if they differ, one or both authors must have gotten the story wrong.

John, at the end of his Gospel, admitted that he had been selective and had not included everything when he wrote:

> Jesus did many other things as well. If every one of them were written down, I suppose that even the whole world would not have room for the books that would be written. (John 21:25)

The last group of supposed contradictions that we will look at concerns numbers. Often these are the hardest contradictions of all to deal with because we have very little information to go on in many cases.

The way that ancient languages like Hebrew and Greek handled numbers made them much more prone to corruption than today. Still, even today, it is not hard to transpose two numbers when copying or inadvertently leave off a zero, etc.

Numbers in Hebrew could be written out in full (two thousand three hundred and forty-five), written as symbols (2345), or written as letters of the alphabet (BCDE). Most of the time, any problems that have occurred in transmission are easily detected.

While the Bible is virtually the same as that written by the apostles and prophets, there remain a few places where the text is uncertain. John Wenham listed some problems that occurred during the transmission of numbers in the Hebrew Scripture:

> We have instances of extra noughts being added to a number: 2 Samuel 10:18 reads '700 chariots,' 1 Chronicles 19:18 reads '7000.' A digit can drop out: 2 Kings 24:8 gives the age of Jehoiachin on accession as 18, whereas 2 Chronicles 36:9 gives it as 8. An entire numeral can drop out: 1 Samuel 13:1 says 'Saul was years old.' In Ezra 2 and Nehemiah 7 the numbers often vary by one unit. And there are other errors of copying many of which are easily explained.[19][14]

---

19 John Wenham, *The Large Numbers of the Old Testament* in *Eerdman's Handbook to the Bible* (Grand Rapids: William B Eerdmans, 1973) pg 191.

In many instances supporting evidence for the correct rendering can be found, often in the Septuagint, and these passages are corrected in most modern translations. For instance, the New International Version translates 2 Chronicles 36:9 as "Jehoiachin was eighteen..." and 1 Samuel 13:1 as "Saul was thirty years old..."

Sometimes it is not completely clear which passage is corrupt. It seems most likely that 2 Samuel 10:18 lost a zero in transmission. Yet, the translators of the New International Version render it as "seven hundred of their charioteers." This translation is because we can't completely rule out the possibility of an additional zero in the number given in 1 Chronicle 19:18.

We can see some problems that can occur with numbers in the Bible in the alleged contradiction concerning the time of the crucifixion. As Burr describes this alleged contradiction:

> CHRIST WAS CRUCIFIED AT THE THIRD HOUR
> And it was the *third hour* and they crucified him. (Mark 15:25)
> CHRIST WAS **NOT** CRUCIFIED UNTIL THE *SIXTH HOUR*
> And it was the preparation of the Passover, and about the *sixth hour*; and he saith unto the Jews, Behold your king... *Shall I crucify* your king? (John 19:14,15)[20]

The question is: How could Jesus have been handed over to be crucified at the sixth hour when he was crucified three hours earlier? Scholars have proposed three possible answers to this problem.

Some have suggested that what we have here is simply a copyist error. Greek was prone to many of the same problems as Hebrew regarding handling numbers. Considering that the Greek numbers 3 (Γ) and 6 ($\digamma$) look similar, especially when handwritten, a copyist error becomes possible. The main problem with this theory is that no such variation has been seen in any ancient manuscripts, so there is no external evidence to support it.

A second possibility is that Mark and John used different methods for telling time. Mark, along with Matthew and Luke,

---

20 William Henry Burr, *Self Contradictions of the Bible* (Buffalo NY: Prometheus Books, 1987) p. 60-61.

used the Jewish method centered around sunrise and sunset. In this method, the hours of the day count from sunrise. Assuming that sunrise occurred at approximately 6:00 A.M., Mark places the crucifixion 3 hours later, or around 9:00 A.M.

On the other hand, John appears to measure time by the Roman method. The Romans measured time the same way we do now, from midnight to midnight.

One indication that John used the Roman system can be seen in the following chapter when he records that the disciples gathered during the evening on the day of the Resurrection.[21] Had John used the Jewish system, the disciples met at the beginning of the next day and not on the evening of the Resurrection.

If it is true that John used the Roman system, while Mark used the Jewish system, then John says that at about the sixth hour (6:00 A.M.) Pilate handed Jesus over to the guards for crucifixion, which Mark says happened at 9:00 A.M. There is no contradiction between these two accounts.

The most likely answer seems to be that this is simply a result of generalization. We must remember that the writers of the Bible did not wear digital watches and did not have a modern concept of accuracy concerning time.

For most of the ancient world, time was reckoned not in hours, minutes, and seconds but only in quarters of a day. This use of time can be seen in the Bible since the only specific times mentioned are the third, sixth, and ninth hours.[22]

Considering this, Mark's reference to the third hour could have meant only the third hour had passed, and it could represent any time between the third and the sixth hour or between 9:00 A.M. and noon.

John said Jesus was handed over "*about the sixth hour,*" which could include the period leading up to noon. Thus, these two state-

---

21   Craig Blomberg, *The Historical Reliability of the Gospels* (Downers Grove, Illinois: Inter-Varsity, 1987) p. 180.

22   John 20:19.

ments are not necessarily in conflict because the times mentioned overlap.

After examining these supposed contradictions, we have seen that they are not contradictions. I chose these particular examples not because they were the easiest to answer but because they are some of the most common.

As for all the other alleged contradictions, their answers are readily available and have been for at least a hundred years.[23] Yet this raises the question: if scholars answered these over a hundred years ago, why are they still being used today? Haley, after his extensive research into supposed contradictions, wrote,

> the more thoroughly I have investigated the subject the more clearly have I seen the flimsy and disingenuous character of the objections alleged.[24]

What can be said is that the Bible does not contradict itself. Many have claimed contradictions. Still, the contradictions disappear when we examine these claims in context, in the original languages, and light of the historical settings. That the Bible is internally consistent in what it says is revealed by the fact that after nearly 2000 years, not a single valid contradiction has been shown to exist between the many various accounts and authors.

TESTS FOR AUTHENTICITY

Beyond being consistent, there are many other internal factors that one can look at when considering the accuracy of an account. One is how early an account is. Strangely enough, this is one area where radical criticism has actually helped the conservative position.

---

23 Two good sources for these answers to alleged problems in the Bible are: John W Haley, *Alleged Discrepancies of the Bible* (Grand Rapids, MI: Baker Books, 1977) and Gleason L. Archer, *Encyclopedia of Bible Difficulties* (Grand Rapids, MI: Regency, 1982).

24 John W Haley, *Alleged Discrepancies of the Bible* (Grand Rapids, MI: Baker Books, 1977) p. x.

One of the areas of study most recently developed by biblical scholars is called redaction criticism. Redaction criticism is the study and analysis of how an author uses sources.

As a result of this research, scholars realized that the New Testament authors wrote very early. Some liberal scholars are now arguing for earlier dates than conservative scholars.[25]

In any event, the majority of liberal and conservative scholars now accept that a significant portion of the New Testament was completed within forty years of the ministry of Jesus.

This short period from the death and resurrection of Jesus Christ until the writing of the New Testament does not leave enough time to create a mythical tradition concerning Jesus. There were simply too many people still alive, both supporters and critics, who would have remembered the events of Jesus' life. We can see this in the New Testament when the apostles used eyewitnesses to support their claims concerning Jesus.[26]

When we examine the individual accounts recorded in the Bible, historians have criteria to judge if they are reliable. When examining the Gospels, there are four tests we can use.[27]

The first test is that of multiple sources. If several Gospels independently recount the same story, then the material in question must have been based on sources, either written or oral, that the writers believed reliable, or they reflect eyewitness accounts.

When the writer of an account uses other sources, these sources must have originated closer to the actual events. The closer to the events, the more likely it is to be accurate. For example, we find the

---

25 The liberal scholar, John A. T. Robinson, argues that John was written before A.D. 70, while most conservative scholars would argue for a date around A.D. 90. He also believed that the entire New Testament had been completed before this date. John A. T. Robinson, *Redating the New Testament* (Philadelphia, PA: Westminster Press, 1976).

26 1 Corinthians 15:3-9 Note in verse 6 that Paul claim many of the 500 eyewitnesses were still alive.

27 Craig Blomberg, The Historical Reliability of the Gospels (Downers Grove, Illinois: Inter-Varsity, 1987) p. 246-48.

parables of Jesus in all the Gospels. There is widespread agreement, even among critics, that these are authentic.

The second test concerns the style of Greek used to record a story. At this point, it is good to remember that Jesus probably did not teach in Greek. When his disciples wrote down or memorized his teachings, a widespread practice during this period, they most likely would not have done so in Greek.

As a result, if the Greek text shows signs of being a translation and/or uses a Semitic style, then the account probably reflects events as disciples recorded them, at or close to, the time they occurred. Only later did they translate these accounts into Greek for the Gospel.

We can see an example of this in the Great Commission (Mathew 28:18). A common Hebrew idiom was the double use of words for speaking to introduce quotes. While many translations smooth this out to correspond with modern English usage, the New American Standard Version preserves this in their translation, "And Jesus came up and **spoke** to them, **saying**,..."[28]

In an article in The Bible Translator, David Alan Black lists 21 types of Semitisms found in the New Testament. He notes that,

> No one who knows Hebrew or another Semitic language can fail to be impressed by the Semitic tone and flavor of the New Testament and its obvious adoption of Semitic modes of speech.[29]

A third test is dissimilarity. This test compares the accounts of Jesus to the expectations for a religious leader during the first century and the early church's beliefs. In short, this test states that if it is unlikely that a disciple would make up a particular story, then they probably didn't.

For example, Jesus referred to God as His Father (*Abba*). His claim would have offended many Jews of his day as blasphemy. Since it is implausible that his disciples would have put these words

---

28   David Alan Black, *New Testament Semitisms, The Bible Translator*, Vol 39 No. 2, April 1988.

29   David Alan Black, *New Testament Semitisms, The Bible Translator*, Vol 39 No. 2, April 1988, p. 216.

on his lips had he not said them, liberal scholars now believe these statements are one of the most authentic parts of the Gospel record.[30]

The final test we will examine is coherence. This test states that if an account fits in well with other accounts determined reliable using one of the other three tests, the account should also be considered reliable. Again, we have found all the accounts present a consistent picture of reliability which, through coherence, end up supporting the overall reliability of the Bible.

CONCLUSION

As biblical scholars have applied these and other historical criteria to the study of the Gospels, the old skeptical beliefs that the accounts contained nothing except myths have crumbled. Rene Latourelle surveyed many critical Gospels studies to see how scholars applied these tests. He found that many of these scholars found large portions of the Gospel accounts authentic, including,

> the linguistic, social, political, economic, cultural and religious environments depicted; the great events of Jesus' life – baptism, temptation, transfiguration, teaching on the kingdom, call to repentance, parables, beatitudes, teaching on God as Father, the miracles and exorcisms as signs of the kingdom, the betrayal, agony, trial, crucifixion, burial and resurrection; the controversies with the Scribes and Pharisees; Jesus' attitudes of simplicity and authority, of purity and compassion; the Christology implied by the sign of Jonah, the sign of the temple and the "Son of man" title; the rejection of a space- or time-bound kingdom; and the calling and mission of the apostles, coupled with their initial enthusiasm, subsequent lack of understanding and final betrayal and desertion.[31]

When applied to the Gospel accounts, we see that these tests show there are sound reasons to consider the Gospel accounts reliable.

30 Craig Blomberg, The Historical Reliability of the Gospels (Downers Grove, Illinois: Inter-Varsity, 1987) p. 251.

31 Craig Blomberg, The Historical Reliability of the Gospels (Downers Grove, Illinois: Inter-Varsity, 1987) p. 253.

Yet if the evidence is so strong, why are they questioned? In short, it is their mention of miracles and other supernatural events. For someone rejecting the possibility of anything supernatural, their very mention automatically renders the account unreliable, regardless of the evidence for reliability.

Still, believing in the unreliability of the account because it mentions the supernatural is an assumption one brings to the text, not a conclusion based on the evidence. The evidence supports reliability.

When applied to the Bible in general, we find similar strong reasons to consider the biblical accounts reliable historical accounts. Looking at the Bible with the same standards we apply to any other ancient historical document, we find ample reasons to accept it as historically accurate. We can say with confidence that the Bible is reliable.

7

THE WORD OF GOD
OR THE
SPECULATIONS OF MEN?

*Above all you must understand that no prophecy of
Scripture came about by the prophet's own interpretation.
(2 Peter 1:20)*

THERE IS A MODERN PARABLE OF A MAN with a strange
affliction. He believed he was dead. Naturally, this caused
great concern to his friends and loved ones, especially his wife.
So one day, his wife asked him to see a doctor. Perhaps the doctor
could convince the man that he was alive.

After examining the man, the doctor decided on a course of
action. He asked the man to learn as much about dead people as
possible. For the next six months, the man studied dead people.

He read all kinds of medical books and magazines. He went
to the morgue and watched autopsies and mortuaries to see bodies
prepared for burial. Soon the man became an expert on the dead.
After six months of investigation, the man returned to the doctor
to discuss his findings.

The doctor asked him, "Do you still think you are dead?"

"Oh yes," the man said. "I have found nothing in my research
that would lead me to believe otherwise."

"I have a question then, do dead people bleed?"

"Absolutely not! All my reading and the autopsies I witnessed
show conclusively that dead people do not bleed."

"You're quite sure of that fact?" the doctor asked.

"Quite sure," the man said confidently.

At this point, the doctor reached into his desk, pulled out a letter opener, and stabbed the man in the arm just hard enough to cause him to bleed. The man sat in stunned silence, staring at the trickle of blood flowing from the wound.

After a few moments, he looked at the doctor and said, "Doctor! Do you know what this means? Dead people do bleed!"

This parable shows that fundamental beliefs are tough to change. Even though the evidence clearly showed that dead people do not bleed, a bleeding arm only convinced this man that the evidence was wrong.

In his popular book on the history of technology, *The Ascent of Man*, Jacob Bronowski wrote that "the Bible is a curious history, part folklore and part record."[1] While this view may be a popular one, it is in direct opposition to the claim made by the apostle Paul when he wrote to his young disciple Timothy:

> All Scripture is God-breathed and is useful for teaching, rebuking, correcting and training in righteousness, so that the man of God may be thoroughly equipped for every good work. (2 Timothy 3:16-17)

Atheists and agnostics often complain that it is unreasonable to base your life on the Bible. They assert that to accept anything simply because it was written down surrenders your rational ability.

One problem with this argument is that to be rational, one must base their views on something and not just pull them out of thin air. Frequently, skeptics will claim that they base their views on reason rather than the Bible. But reason is a process, not a foundation. It is a way of thinking about things and not itself a foundation for belief.[2]

For example, Christian morality comes from the Bible. Applying reason to the moral principles of the Bible, Christians can reach conclusions about moral issues.

---

1   Jacob Bronowski, *The Ascent of Man* (Boston: Little, Brown and Company, 1973) p. 72.

2   See Elgin Hushbeck, *Seeking Truth: How to Move From Partisan Bickering to Building Consensus* (Gonzalez, Florida: Energion, 2022).

Yet, what is the foundation an atheist uses? To what do they apply reason to reach a conclusion? Where do they derive their moral principles upon which to apply reason? There seems to be no clear answer. While atheists and agnostics may be critical of Christian foundations, at least Christians have a foundation. More importantly, this criticism ignores the most crucial part of the Christian's belief concerning the Bible.

Implicit in the skeptic's argument is the unstated belief that the Bible is simply the product of men. If this were true, if the Bible were only the writings of men containing their thoughts on religion, then the skeptics would have a valid point. In that case, we should treat the Bible as any other book, and it would hold no special status.

The Christian position, however, is that the Bible is not just the speculative writings of men. As the apostle Peter tells us:

> For prophecy never had its origin in the will of man, but men spoke from God as they were carried along by the Holy Spirit (2 Peter 1:21).

At the heart of the Christian's claims concerning the Bible is the belief that it is the inspired word of God.

Christians do not subjugate their reason simply to a book but to the word of God. They don't believe it just because someone wrote it down long ago but because they believe God inspires these words. In other words, Christians are not trusting a book; they trust God.

Therefore, the real question is: Is the Bible the word of God? As we saw, the Bible is clear on this question. Often skeptics object to claims such as Paul's that God inspires all scripture because Christians use the Bible to prove the Bible. In short, they are using circular reasoning.

This criticism is valid for those few Christians who basically argue, 'The Bible says it is the word of God; therefore, it must be the word of God.' But this does not affect those who do not make such simplistic arguments.

This argument also neglects that a single author did not write the Bible. The book that we call the Bible contains many separate books. It is a collection of sixty-six books written by over forty people during approximately 1500 years.

The only way the circular reasoning argument could be considered valid is if one accepts that the authors were all inspired by a single source, God. But this would require the critic to accept the very point they are trying to disprove.

The authors of the Bible serve as independent witnesses, all claiming to have had an experience with God. That they support each other in their belief in a personal God is no more an example of circular reasoning than one scientist quoting another to support a theory.

While the consistent testimony of over forty witnesses is strong evidence, it does not, in and of itself, show that the Bible is the word of God. There is, of course, the possibility that all forty could be wrong.

So, is there any other evidence to support the divine inspiration of the Bible? We could only say God inspired the Bible if it contained something that no human could have written. While this may initially seem impossible, it is not that difficult to demonstrate.

TEST EVERYTHING

Contrary to popular opinion, the Bible does not ask Christians to accept everything on blind faith. One theme constantly stressed throughout the Bible is questioning and testing claims.

If someone claims God sent them, we are not just to believe everything they say. When someone claims to have a message from God, we must first test the claim.

The apostle Paul urged the early believers in the church at Thessalonica to "Test everything. Hold on to the good. Avoid every kind of evil" (1 Thessalonians 5:21,22). Similarly, the apostle John wrote.

> Dear friends, do not believe every spirit, but test
> the spirits to see whether they are from God, because
> many false prophets have gone out into the world...
> They are from the world and therefore speak from the
> viewpoint of the world, and the world listens to them.
> (1 John 4:1,5)

The Christians who lived in the city of Berea were praised because they did not blindly accept what the apostle Paul had told them. Luke wrote of the Bereans that they,

> were of more noble character than the Thes-
> salonians, for they received the message with great
> eagerness and examined the Scriptures every day to
> see if what Paul said was true. (Acts 17:11)

God has never asked that we blindly accept his messages. Instead, He has consistently warned us to be on our guard against false prophets.

In his final speech to the people of Israel before they entered the promised land, Moses said that God would send prophets who would deliver his messages. Still, the people must beware of the false prophets who would also come.

> The LORD said to me: "What they say is good. I
> will raise for them a prophet like you from among their
> brothers: I will put my words in his mouth, and he will
> tell them everything I command him. If anyone does
> not listen to my words that the prophet speaks in my
> name, I myself will call him to account. But a prophet
> who presumes to speak in my name anything I have not
> commanded him to say, or a prophet who speaks in the
> name of other gods, must be put to death." (Deuteron-
> omy 18:17-20)

How does one tell the difference between a prophet of God and a false prophet? Moses explains:

> You may say to yourselves, "How can we know
> when a message has not been spoken by the LORD?" If
> what a prophet proclaims in the name of the LORD does
> not take place or come true, that is a message the LORD
> has not spoken. That prophet has spoken presumptu-
> ously. Do not be afraid of him. (Deuteronomy 18:21,22)

God has warned us to beware of those who would claim to be from Him but who are false prophets. So that we would be able to tell the difference between a prophet sent by God and a false prophet, God included in his messages things that no human could possibly know: predictions concerning the future. If a prophet claims to speak for God and predicts the future, and what they say does not occur, then they are a false prophet.[3]

This test is still valid today. If the Bible contains predictions that are beyond the ability of human knowledge, the logical conclusion is that God inspired it. All we need to show is that the Bible contains at least one prediction of the future, which could not have come through human means or a lucky guess to establish its divine inspiration.[4]

The Bible contains not just one but hundreds, if not thousands, of prophecies concerning the future. Almost all of these prophecies, except those dealing with the end times, have already come to pass with astonishing accuracy.

These prophecies are so accurate that even the skeptics have noted them. Yet, rather than accept the conclusion that God inspired the Bible, the skeptic looks for another explanation.

Skeptics handle prophecy in one of two ways. The first is to write off biblical prophecy as being so vague that it could apply to many situations. Thus when there is a correlation between a prophecy and an event, it is not all that surprising. The skeptic would claim that the prophecy could be interpreted to fit many events.

While this explanation might work for some prophecies, many are too specific. The prophet Isaiah wrote around 700 B.C. not

---

3   A second test is that the message must be in agreement with what
     God has taught in the past, for God cannot contradict Himself.
     (Deuteronomy 13:1-3).

4   The existence of such a prophecy would not strictly demonstrate divine
     inspiration by God. One could, for example, claim that the information
     came from an extraterrestrial being from the planet Gallifrey. The
     alternatives to God, however, are highly unlikely and thus will not be
     dealt with directly.

only of Israel's restoration but that it would occur under the ruler-ship of a king named Cyrus (Isaiah 44:28).

This prophecy is not a generalized one that could fit many situations. At the time, Israel was not even in captivity and thus did not need restoration. Yet 150 years later, it happened just as Isaiah said it would. Many of the Bible's prophecies are specific enough to leave little doubt concerning their fulfillment.

The second explanation acknowledges that the prophecies in the Bible are very accurate in their predictions. Many skeptics even agree with Christians that these prophecies are much too accurate and specific to come by human means.

They do not, however, say that these prophecies came from God. Instead, they say these prophecies are so accurate that they could not be prophecies at all; they are history. In other words, the reason these prophecies are so accurate is they were written down *after* the events they 'predict.'

Isaiah was able to predict that a ruler named Cyrus would allow the Jews to return from Babylon because a different person, a second Isaiah, who lived and wrote after Cyrus issued his decree, wrote that section of the book.

The nice part about this argument for skeptics is that this is very hard to disprove for many prophecies. The primary reason for most predictions was to validate that the prophet was indeed from God. Because of this, the prophecies were often of events that would happen shortly, either during the prophet's lifetime or shortly after their death.

Often, the time between a prophecy and its fulfillment was only a matter of a few months or years. It is tough today to show with any degree of certainty that these prophecies were written before the events they predicted.

Regardless of the other methods available for dating a book, for the skeptic, the existence of an accurate prophecy, in and of itself, is evidence enough to assign a later date to a book. After reviewing the evidence put forth by liberal scholars concerning the date of the Gospel of Matthew, Isaac Asimov concluded that,

> Little can be said as to the time when Matthew was
> written. From the references to the destruction of the
> Temple, which are found in various places in the gospel,
> it is often suggested that the book reached its present
> form shortly after the fateful year of A.D. 70.[5]

Yet, in each place in Matthew where the temple's destruction is mentioned, it is clearly a prophecy of an event that had not occurred.

Thankfully, not all of the prophecies in the Bible are short-ranged. At times God does reveal part of his overall plan. Some of these prophecies were fulfilled long after the death of the prophet. The longer the period of time between a prophecy and its fulfillment, the easier it is to show that the prophecy came first. To avoid the question of postdating, we will examine only those prophecies where there is no question that they came before the events they predict.

KORAZIN, BETHSAIDA AND CAPERNAUM

Jesus gave one such prophecy during his ministry around the Sea of Galilee. The people in three of the four cities by the Sea rejected Jesus, even though he had performed many miracles. Because of this,

> Jesus began to denounce the cities in which most
> of his miracles had been performed, because they did
> not repent. "Woe to you, Korazin! Woe to you, Beth-
> saida! If the miracles that were performed in you had
> been performed in Tyre and Sidon, they would have re-
> pented long ago in sackcloth and ashes. But I tell you,
> it will be more bearable for Tyre and Sidon on the day
> of judgment than for you. And you Capernaum, will be
> lifted up to the depths. If the miracles that were per-
> formed in you had been performed in Sodom, it would
> have remained to this day. But I tell you that it will be
> more bearable for Sodom on the day of judgment than
> for you." (Matthew 11:20-24)

---

5   Isaac Asimov, *Asimov's Guide to the Bible, The New Testament* (New York: Avon Books, 1969) p. 109.

Here Jesus compares the fate of three cities to three cities well known to his audience for falling under God's judgment. Two of these cities were wiped entirely out of existence.

Most people know the judgment of fire and brimstone wiping out Sodom, along with Gomorrah, recorded in Genesis (Genesis 19:1-29). The fate of Tyre is perhaps not as well known.

Tyre was once one of the largest and most influential cities in that region of the Mediterranean. To Tyre, God said that judgment would come and destroy the city. Tyre was not simply to be conquered or abandoned, but as recorded by the prophet Ezekiel:

> This is what the Sovereign LORD says: I am against you, O Tyre, and I will bring many nations against you, like the sea casting up its waves. They will destroy the walls of Tyre and pull down her towers; I will scrape away her rubble and make her a bare rock... they will break down your walls and demolish your fine houses and throw your stones, timber and rubble into the sea... you will become a place to spread fish nets. You will never be rebuilt. (Ezekiel 26:3-4, 12, 14)

Many nations did attack Tyre. Nebuchadnezzar attacked the city in 586 B.C., shortly after this prophecy. Before he could capture the city, virtually the entire population moved to a small island about half a mile off the coast and out of Nebuchadnezzar's reach. Before he left, Nebuchadnezzar showed his anger by destroying the main city.

A little over 250 years later, Tyre was once again attacked, this time by Alexander the Great. But Alexander had a problem. The remaining city was on an island, and he did not have a fleet to reach it.

When the people of Tyre refused to surrender, Alexander ordered his men to dismantle the ruins of the old city destroyed by Nebuchadnezzar. They then used this material to build a causeway out to the island so Alexander could attack. In the process, the old city was literally removed down to the bare rock and thrown into the sea.

Today, nothing remains at the site of the ancient Tyre but a small fishing village. The fishermen did at one time use the area cleared by Alexander's men to dry their nets, and Tire never again rose to such a position of power.

Concerning the fate of the three cities denounced by Jesus, Capernaum lasted until the beginning of the fifth century when an earthquake destroyed it. Korazin and Bethsaida also disappeared about this time.

A fourth city on the sea of Galilee at the time of Jesus' ministry was the city of Tiberias. Jesus did not include this city in the prophecy. While Tiberias was partially destroyed many times, it has always been rebuilt and is still a vibrant city today.

Jesus denounced three cities by comparing them to cities previously destroyed under God's judgment. They were destroyed and never rebuilt, and the city He did not condemn remains to this day.

While skeptics usually try to post-date prophecies to eliminate any necessity of supernatural influence, this is not an option for this prophecy. The destruction of these cities did not occur until the fifth century A.D. Yet we have copies of the prophecy going back to the second century A.D. There is absolutely no doubt that this prophecy happened hundreds of years before the events it predicted took place.

ISRAEL

Two of the most long-ranged prophecies in the Bible concern the people of Israel. Before they entered the land God gave them, He warned the Jewish people about the consequences of disobedience. God said that should the people of Israel ever forsake Him and His commandments, He would punish them. If they continued to rebel against Him, God told them the following,

> If in spite of this you still do not listen to me but continue to be hostile towards me, then in my anger I will be hostile towards you... I will turn your cities into ruins and lay waste your sanctuaries, and I will take no delight in the pleasing aroma of your offerings. I will lay waste the land, so that your enemies who live there will be appalled. I will scatter you among the nations and will draw out my sword and pursue you. Your land will

> be laid waste, and your cities will lie in ruins (Leviticus 26:27-8, 31-33).

If the Jewish people ever rejected God, He would destroy their cities and the temple, forcing them out of the land. Jesus also predicted the coming destruction of the temple when he said,

> As for what you see here, the time will come when not one stone will be left on another; every one of them will be thrown down (Luke 21:6).

As to the impending destruction of Jerusalem, Jesus warned his disciples:

> When you see Jerusalem being surrounded by armies, you will know that its desolation is near. Then let those who are in Judea flee to the mountains, let those in the city get out, and let those in the country not enter the city. For this is the time of punishment in fulfillment of all that has been written. (Luke 21:20-22)

The complete fulfillment of these prophecies came a little over one hundred years after the rejection of Jesus as the Messiah.

In A.D. 66, the Jews, tired of the repressive rule of Rome, declared their independence. Emperor Nero was not amused and sent an army led by Vespasian to stop the rebellion. When Vespasian, upon the death of Nero, became emperor in A.D. 69, he left the task of quelling the rebellion to his son Titus.

By A.D. 70, Titus and his army had recaptured the city of Jerusalem, virtually destroying the city in the process. Josephus writes concerning the siege:

> Now, as soon as the army had no more people to slay or to plunder, because there remained none to be objects of their fury (for they would not have spared any, had there remained any other such work to be done) Caesar gave orders that they should now demolish the entire city and temple.[6]

---

6   Flavius Josephus, *The Works of Flavius Josephus* Trans. William Whiston, Vol. 1 *Wars of the Jews* VII I I (Grand Rapids, MI: Baker Books, 1979) p. 473.

Jesus' prophecy that one stone would not be left on another was literally fulfilled. During the siege, soldiers set the temple on fire, and the fire caused the gold leaf adorning the roof to melt and flow into the cracks between the blocks. The temple was dismantled stone by stone to retrieve the gold. Once they had the gold, they threw the stones into the valley.

The remaining Jewish rebels, now all but defeated, retreated to the stronghold of Masada. This move was a futile gesture. Within three years, Masada had also fallen, and the rebellion ended. A second rebellion broke out in A.D. 132 and lasted for three years before it also was put down.

This time the Romans were even more severe. Those captured during the rebellion were either sold into slavery or executed. The Romans banned the Jewish religion and prohibited Jews from even going near Jerusalem. As a final insult, the land was renamed Palestine after the historical enemies of the Jews.

The prophecy given in Leviticus was fulfilled entirely 1400 years later. After the rejection of Jesus, Israel's cities were devastated, and the people were driven out of the land given to them by God.

God, however, was not done with the nation of Israel. The prophet Ezekiel gave a series of prophecies revealing God's ultimate plans for the Jewish people. He said:

> This is what the Sovereign LORD says: On the day I cleanse you from all your sins, I will resettle your towns, and the ruins will be rebuilt. The desolate land will be cultivated instead of lying desolate in the sight of all who pass through it. They will say, "This land that was laid waste has become like the garden of Eden; the cities that were lying in ruins, desolate and destroyed, are now fortified and inhabited." Then the nations around you that remain will know that I the LORD have rebuilt what was destroyed and have replanted what was desolate. I the LORD have spoken, and I will do it. (Ezekiel 36:33-36)

This prophecy is part of a more extensive series of prophecies concerning events occurring near the end times. As Ralph Alexander, Professor of Hebrew Scriptures at Western Seminary wrote in his commentary on the book of Ezekiel:

> The entire context of these six messages was future. The context of chapters 36-37, before and following this apocalyptic vision, indicates that Israel's national restoration in the end time was in view.[7]

Ezekiel predicted that at some time in the distant future, God would gather the Jewish people and place them again in the land of Israel. The land would remain desolate until their return, but it would once again become productive.

The fulfillment of this prophecy can hardly be questioned. After the Romans expelled the Jews, the land of Israel remained in a state of desolation for over 1800 years. For this entire period, the Jewish people remained as an entity surviving apart from a homeland.

Then in 1948, after almost 2000 years, the Jews returned to their ancient homeland. In the short span of 40 years, and under challenging conditions, what had been little more than a desert became a major agricultural producer exporting food to Europe.

The restoration of Israel is truly a miraculous event that can hardly be overestimated. It is a miracle in and of itself that the Jewish people were able to survive all of this time as an identifiable unit. No other group expelled from their land continued as an identifiable group for even a few hundred years, much less the nearly 2000 years that the Jews had existed without a homeland.

Scattered across many nations, that they could organize a homeland in the same area as their original country would be inconceivable had it not already happened.

This is precisely what people thought during the nineteenth and early twentieth century. Some commentators, referring to the prophecies concerning the restoration of Israel, considered them allegorical, mystical, or for skeptics, just plain wrong. The idea that

---

7   Ralph H Alexander, *Ezekiel* in *The Expositor's Bible Commentary Vol. 6* ed. Frank E Gaebelein (Grand Rapids, MI: Zondervan, 1986) p. 926.

the Jewish people would be able to form a nation after nearly 2000 years was beyond comprehension.

Sir Robert Anderson was the Assistant Commissioner of the Metropolitan Police and Chief of the Criminal Investigations Department during the Jack the Ripper murders. He was also an author who noted this skepticism in his book on the end times, *The Coming Prince*. During the 1880s, when the idea of a restored Israel seemed an impossible dream, Anderson wrote :

> The minds of most men are in bondage to the commonplace facts of their experience. The prophecies of a restored Israel seem to many as incredible as predictions of the present triumphs of electricity and steam would have appeared to our ancestors a century ago.[8]

Anderson believed the word of God could be trusted, and so wrote:

> But Israel's history has yet to be completed; and when that nation comes again upon the scene, the element of miraculous interpositions will mark once more the course of events on earth... Judah shall again become a nation, Jerusalem shall be restored, and that temple shall be built in which the "abomination of desolation" is to stand.[9]

Anderson made this statement based on the prophecies in the Bible, sixty-four years before Israel became a nation.

Now that the Jews have returned to Israel, critics ignore the context of the prophecy. They claim that the restoration does not refer to a future restoration during the end times. Instead, it is the return of Israel from Babylonian captivity.

While this explanation may satisfy skeptics seeking to remove all supernatural influence from the Bible, it presents a number of problems. First and foremost is that this interpretation goes against the clear sense of the text, which is the distant future. There is a

---

8   Sir Robert Anderson, *The Coming Prince* (Grand Rapids, MI: Kregel, 1984) p. 150.

9   Sir Robert Anderson, *The Coming Prince* (Grand Rapids, MI: Kregel, 1984) p. 167, 170.

Evidence for the Bible   193

reason people like Anderson defended these prophecies when so many thought the idea of a restored Israel absurd.

The prophecy given by Ezekiel fits the modern restoration of Israel. Are we to believe that it is all just a coincidence? Is it just luck that Ezekiel (and other prophets) predicted a restoration of Israel in the distant future and that Israel was restored as a nation 2500 years later?

THE MINISTRY OF CHRIST

One of the most common criticisms of biblical prophecy is that it is not specific enough. The prophecies mentioned above, while quite specific, were still vague in one area. These prophecies did not specify a time frame.

While what would happen was predicted, when these events would occur was not mentioned. For a prophecy that is specific in both the event it predicts, and the time the event will happen, we will examine the book of Daniel.

Daniel is one of the most prophetic books in the Hebrew Scriptures and, therefore, one of the most controversial. The prophecies in Daniel are so accurate that liberal scholars have long tried to date this book as late as possible.

Because of this, the date assigned by most liberal scholars is around 165 B.C., the time of the Maccabean revolt against Antiochus Epiphanes. Daniel cannot be dated any later than this because of copies found among the Dead Sea Scrolls.

Conservative scholars have long since refuted the arguments for a later date suggested by liberal scholars.[10] They have also pointed out several problems such a late date would cause.

For instance, while common during the sixth century B.C., many of the terms in Daniel were no longer used during the period, liberal scholars suggest for the book. The translators of the Sep-

---

10   Gleason L Archer, *A Survey of Old Testament Introduction* (Chicago: Moody Press, 1974) pp. 385-411.
      Josh McDowell, *Daniel in the Critics' Den* (San Bernardino, CA: Here's Life, 1979).

tuagint version of Daniel, done at about the time liberal scholars dated the book, could not translate many of these terms correctly.

If written around 165 B.C., how did Daniel's writer know the proper Babylon terminology in use 350 years earlier, yet the scholars who translated Daniel into Greek at roughly the same time did not?

Still, the real problem is that even a date as late as 165 B.C. does not solve all the problems. This is because many of the prophecies were fulfilled long after 165 B.C. One example is a vision that Daniel received concerning the seventy "weeks."

Daniel wrote during the Babylonian captivity when many Jews lived in Babylon. Daniel read in the writings of Jeremiah a prophecy that stated that the exile would last for seventy years (Jeremiah 25:11-13).

The exile had occurred in several stages, and Daniel was unsure when the seventy years started. He prayed that the exile would end as soon as possible.

While Daniel was praying, the angel Gabriel visited him, sent to give him further understanding concerning the eventual history of the Jewish people. Gabriel told Daniel:

> Know and understand this: From the issuing of the decree to restore and rebuild Jerusalem until the Anointed One, the ruler, comes, there will be seven 'sevens,' and sixty-two 'sevens.' It will be rebuilt with streets and a trench, but in times of trouble. After the sixty-two 'sevens,' the Anointed One will be cut off and will have nothing. The people of the ruler who will come will destroy the city and the sanctuary. (Daniel 9:25-26)

The word translated as "sevens" is the Hebrew word *heptads*, which literally means *groups of seven*. Translators often render this as "weeks." Both liberal and conservative scholars agree that the "weeks" here are groups of seven years.

The first period consists of seven "sevens," or forty-nine years, during which the Jews will rebuild the city of Jerusalem. Then there will be the second period of sixty-two "sevens," or 434 years, after which will come the Anointed One.

The term "Anointed One" is the Hebrew word *Messiah*, which in Greek is *Christ*. Gabriel is telling Daniel that after 483 years (49 + 434), the Messiah will come, but that he will be cut off or killed. After the death of the Anointed One, the city of Jerusalem and the temple will be destroyed.

The critical question becomes: When do the 483 years begin? Gabriel was quite specific on this point. The 483 years were to begin when a decree was issued allowing for rebuilding the city of Jerusalem.

We know that there were four decrees issued regarding the restoration of Jerusalem. Cyrus gave the first decree in the year 539 B.C. This decree was only for the rebuilding of the temple and was not for the rebuilding of Jerusalem itself.

A second decree was issued by Darius twenty years later in 519 B.C. Still, it only reaffirmed the first decree given by Cyrus. In 457 B.C., Artaxerxes sent Ezra to Jerusalem with a third decree. This decree also did not directly provide for the rebuilding of Jerusalem.

Still, it did specify that Ezra take money back to finish the temple. After finishing the temple, Ezra "may then do *whatever seems best with the rest of the silver and gold*" (Ezra 7:18). Ezra said that this decree had

> granted us life to rebuild the house of our God and repair its ruins, and he has given us a wall of protection in Judah and Jerusalem (Ezra 9:9).

That Ezra intended to rebuild the city wall is seen in Nehemiah's disappointment when, a few years later, he learned the wall remained unfinished.

Artaxerxes also gave the fourth decree, but this time to Nehemiah. This decree, issued in 446 B.C., was to finish rebuilding Jerusalem, which Ezra had not completed. Again, that this decree was to finish the rebuilding implies it started with Artaxerxes' previous decree.

Many conservative scholars believe the decree mentioned in Daniel is the first decree of Artaxerxes. Archeologists date this decree in the spring of 457 B.C.

The prophecy in Daniel says that Jerusalem will be rebuilt within forty-nine years from this date, or by 409 B.C., which it was. The Messiah should then appear around A.D. 27 (483 - 457 = 26 + 1 [no year zero] = 27).

The generally accepted time for the crucifixion of Jesus is in the spring of A.D. 30. Allowing for the traditional time for the ministry of Jesus, which was three and one-half years, would mean that the prophecy in Daniel matches perfectly with the life of Jesus Christ.

Daniel predicted that the Messiah would appear around A.D. 27 and that he would die shortly after that. Daniel predicts that Jerusalem and the temple will be destroyed after the Messiah's death. As we have seen, this happened in A.D. 70.

Even if, for the sake of argument, we accept the later date critics claim, this would still mean that Daniel predicted the ministry of Jesus over 190 years before it occurred. Daniel predicts the destruction of Jerusalem and the Temple over 230 years before their destruction.

What do liberal scholars have to say about this prophecy? For the most part, they try to force it into a framework of the Maccabean revolt. John Hayes, Professor of the Old Testament at Emory University, wrote concerning this prophecy,

> From the going forth of the word till the coming of an anointed one was to be seven weeks, or 49 years. The number 586 (the date of the fall of Jerusalem and the beginning of its desolation) minus 49 equals 537, the time of the downfall of Babylon and the decree to return and rebuild Jerusalem under Shesh-bazzar (or Zerub-babel?). The next period was to be 62 weeks or 434 years, but here he seems to have used the fixed point of 605 B.C.[11]

One almost has to wonder if Hayes is referring to the same prophecy. The quotation above contains many problems. First, in an attempt to avoid Daniel's clear reference to Christ, Hayes

---

11   John H. Hayes, *Introduction to the Bible* (Philadelphia, Penn: Westminster Press, 1971) pp. 287-8.

claims that Daniel only predicted that *an* anointed one (Messiah) would appear.

In Hebrew, proper names, and titles used as proper names, do not have definite articles (the), just as in English, we say "Jesus" and not "the Jesus." So from a purely grammatical point of view, this prophecy could refer to either *an* anointed one or to *the* anointed one.

The context, however, demands that it be translated as "the anointed one." If Daniel refers only to "an anointed one," the prophecy would be meaningless, for it could refer to almost any governor or priest-king.

It would be like someone predicting with great fanfare that the next presidential election will elect a president. True, but why all the fanfare? Why is there such a specific time period, and why is this particular anointed one singled out? The prophecy makes much better sense referring to the Messiah.

Another problem is Hayes' claim that the anointed one (Messiah) would appear 49 years after the fall of Jerusalem. The Messiah was not to come forty-nine years after the destruction of Jerusalem, but seven 'sevens' and sixty-two 'sevens' after the decree to rebuild the city.

A third problem is Hayes' statement that Daniel "seems" to have started the 62 'sevens' in 605 B.C. Why 605 B.C.? The only reason Hayes gives is that 434 years after 605 B.C. would have been 171 B.C. At that time, Onias III was murdered. Again, this claim seems to totally ignore what Daniel was saying to force the prophecy to fit Hayes' presuppositions.

Samuel Sandmel also sees a similar interpretation of this prophecy. He writes,

> How are these strange numbers to be interpreted? Possibly the 490 years begin in 586. The first segment may end in 516 with Joshua, the priest contemporary with Zerubbabel at the time of the return of the Jews from Babylonia. The sixty-two weeks, or 434 years, may

begin in 516 and terminate in 171, when Onias III was
slain by Menelaus.[12]

While this may be the standard explanation of this prophecy
suggested by liberal scholars and critics, Sandmel admits that it,

> is scarcely consistent with the arithmetic involved.
> The arithmetic is an insurmountable problem, especially
> since we do not know for sure what the author intends
> as a beginning date, nor can we be sure that his chronol-
> ogy agrees with that accepted by modern scholars. If
> we ignore the mathematical difficulty, we may possibly
> explain the intent.[13]

The real problem is that liberal scholars can only have a
non-supernatural explanation for prophecy. They must relate this
prophecy to the Maccabean revolt, which they believe to be the
book's subject, even if it doesn't fit the prophecy.

We have two explanations for this prophecy. One is that Daniel predicted the time of the coming of Jesus Christ, his death,
and the subsequent destruction of Jerusalem and the temple. This
explanation matches both the prophecy and history perfectly. Its
only problem is that it cannot be explained by natural means.

The other explanation is that the prophecy refers to the Maccabean revolt. While a natural explanation, even those who support
it admit that it does not match the prophecy very well.

When we consider that liberal scholars claim this 'prophecy'
was written shortly after the events, the inconsistencies between the
events and the prophecy are difficult to justify. Because of this, we
must reject the Maccabean interpretation. The only explanation
that fits all the facts is that Daniel accurately predicted the ministry
of Jesus Christ hundreds of years before it occurred.

---

12   Samuel Sandmel, *The Hebrew Scriptures, An Introduction to Their
     Literature and Religious Ideas* (New York: Oxford University Press, 1978)
     p. 234.

13   Samuel Sandmel, *The Hebrew Scriptures, An Introduction to Their
     Literature and Religious Ideas* (New York: Oxford University Press, 1978)
     p. 234.

CONCLUSION

We examined a few of the prophecies in the Bible that clearly predate the events they predict. The events of these prophecies happened just as the prophets said they would. How was this possible?

How could Daniel predict the year in which the ministry of Jesus would begin? Is it reasonable to write this off simply as a guess or luck? A single correct prophecy might be a lucky guess. But every prophecy in the Bible, except those that deal with the last days, has come to pass. Can such accuracy be written off as simply luck?

Some have attempted to apply the principles of probability to biblical prophecy. While attempting to apply exact probabilities to historical events is difficult, we can, at least, get a general idea of the probability for a given event from studying history.

One such study was done by Peter Stoner, Professor Emeritus of Science at Westmont College, and Robert Newman, Associate Professor of Physics and Mathematics at Shelton College.

Stoner and Newman broke down the prophecies they examined into specific events. They then assigned a probability to each part of the prophecy. Once they assign the probabilities, they could use standard probability theory to obtain a probability for the entire prophecy.

For the prophecy concerning the Jews being expelled from Israel and then returning, Stoner and Newman gave the following breakdown in the probabilities,[14]

A)	Cities will be in ruin	Odds 1 in 10
B)	Sanctuary destroyed	Odds 1 in 2
C)	Land laid waste	Odds 1 in 10
D)	Land given to enemies	Odds 1 in 2
E)	Jews scattered among nations	Odds 1 in 5
F)	Persecution	Odds 1 in 10
G)	Jews return to Land	Odds 1 in 10

---

14 Peter Stoner and Robert Newman, *Science Speaks* (Chicago: Moody Press, 1976) pp. 89-90.

While there may be some room for minor adjustments, these probabilities are reasonable overall. If anything, they are somewhat on the low side.

To obtain the overall probability for the prediction, you multiply the individual probabilities. The overall probability, or the likelihood that this prediction happened by chance alone, would be 1 in 20,000.

Stoner and Newman compiled the probabilities for eleven of the prophecies recorded in the Bible. When they calculated the probability that all eleven could have occurred based on chance, the odds were an incredible 1 in 5.76×10^{59}, which is a 1 followed by 59 zeros.[15]

The odds against the fulfillment of just eleven of the prophecies in the Bible are so enormous as to be literally incomprehensible. This list does not include many other prophecies, like Daniel's prediction of the start of Jesus' ministry, the probability of which would be impossible to calculate. According to Stoner and Newman:

> Some will say that the estimates given in some of these prophecies are too large and should be reduced. Others may say that some of the prophecies are related and should have smaller estimates. That may be true, so I would suggest that such a person go back over the prophecies and make his own estimates. They will be found to be still large enough to be conclusive.[16]

These prophecies cannot have occurred by human means alone. They can't be explained away as chance or luck. They were not written after the fact and did not happen from any known natural means.

In the prophecies of the Bible, we have something that no human could have written on their own. The only position left is that the knowledge required for these prophecies came from a

---

15 Peter Stoner and Robert Newman, *Science Speaks* (Chicago: Moody Press, 1976) pp. 95.

16 Peter Stoner and Robert Newman, *Science Speaks* (Chicago: Moody Press, 1976) pp. 95.

source that is not bound by time; from a source that knows the future. In other words, these prophecies came from God.

In this book, we have examined the criticisms of the Bible and found them lacking. We examined the evidence for the text of the Bible and found the text to be thoroughly reliable. We looked at the development of the canon and found, despite critics' claims, that it was an issue settled long before the first Church Councils ever met.

We saw the critiques of modern critics as flawed and based more on their presuppositions than the evidence. We saw that the evidence of archeology backs up the writers' statements in many places.

We looked at the problems with religion, in general, and the Bible that emerged due to modern science. We saw that there was no inherent conflict and that more recent scientific findings lent some support to the Bible in many ways.

We examined the standard tests for assessing the historical reliability of the ancient documents and found that when applied to the Bible, the Bible is a reliable document. Finally, this chapter looked at the Bible's prophecies to see that they are accurate and genuinely the inspired Word of God.

As such, the issue is not whether you can trust the Bible but whether you will trust what God has revealed through the Bible. The choice is yours.

INDEX

www.ingramcontent.com/pod-product-compliance
Lightning Source LLC
Chambersburg PA
CBHW021226090426
42740CB00006B/398